CAUTION.

TO AVOID RISK of suffocation, remember to breathe while reading this book.

Do not read this book under water without approved breathing equipment.

Do not operate motor vehicles or heavy machinery while reading this book.

Do not hit yourself on the head repeatedly with a mallet while reading this book. Once will usually suffice.

Do not start an argument about any controversial subject mentioned in this book with anyone who is visibly larger or better armed than you are.

Always remember, safety first. If you are in any doubt, *do not read this book at all.*

ERRATA.

P. 58. For "Balaclava," read "baklava." Adjust other instructions accordingly.

P. 103. For "arsenic," read "allspice."

P. 171. Add the word "not" thus: "Baking soda is *not* a good substitute for salt in case of scarcity."

Please ignore all text on *pp. 238-253.* When we wrote this chapter, we had just finished Chapter 17, "Know Your Wines and Spirits," and frankly we ended up saying a few things about snow peas that, in the cold light of dawn, we can see ought to have been left unsaid.

P. 285. For "eggs," read "flour." For "broccoli," read "pitted cherries." For "cheese," read "sugar." For "sausage," read "butter." For "pan," read "oven." For "omelet," read "pie."

P. 317. It turns out that nightshade is poisonous. Who would have thought?

P. 389. The page numbers in the index are incorrect. You may easily arrive at the correct page number by remembering that the index assumes that the pages are numbered *logarithmically* rather than *sequentially.*

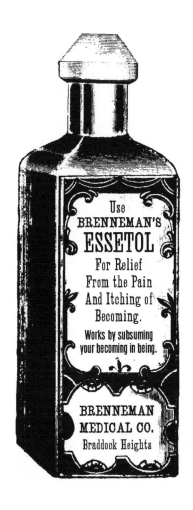

DR. BOLI'S GIFT HORSE.

DR. BOLI'S GIFT HORSE

A CHOICE COLLECTION

From the Pages of **DR. BOLI'S CELEBRATED MAGAZINE.**

PITTSBURGH:
Dr. Boli's Celebrated Publishing Empire
MMXIII.

TABLE OF CONTENTS.

DR. BOLI'S GIFT HORSE.

THE GOOD OLD DAYS.

"TELL ME AGAIN about the old days, grandmother," said the sweet little girl sitting by the fire.

"Well," her grandmother began, her eyes misting over with nostalgia, "we didn't have trees or any of these modern conveniences. When we wanted wood, we had to make it ourselves. I remember the day old Mitch from down at the mill told your great-grandpappy that there was a new kind of plant that grew wood in its stem, and all you had to do was take it if you wanted it. Pappy laughed himself sick. That was how he died, in fact.

"We had to walk fifteen miles in the snow just to get to school, and then when we got there we had to turn around and walk right back, because schools hadn't been invented yet.

"The sun didn't start automatically every morning the way it does now. Pappy had to turn a crank, and some mornings it took forever to get it started. Those were cold mornings, but all we could do was shiver until Pappy got the sun started, because of course no one had thought of blankets in those days.

"The moon was a bit smaller then, and more rectangular. There weren't nearly as many stars, but then we lived in a poor neighborhood. We didn't know we were poor, though, because poverty wasn't discovered till I was eighteen years old. I remember that day, and how cheated we all felt when we finally found out we were poor.

"We didn't have opposable thumbs back then, either. When we wanted to pick something up, we had to use our toes, so of course we fell down a lot. We couldn't hold cups, so we had to drink everything through a straw, even hot water, which we couldn't make into tea or coffee because no one had thought of those things.

"People didn't live very long in those days, either. The average life-span was about twenty-one. I myself died when I was nineteen, but I didn't like it and gave it up after a while. Most people died of starvation, because food hadn't been invented yet, and the only time we ate anything was when something accidentally fell into our mouths."

"Goodness, grandmother," said the little girl, "aren't you glad you lived to see our modern world, with all its wonderful inventions?"

"Well, I'm not so sure I am," the kindly old lady replied. "We had to work hard in the old days, but that made us tough. We didn't have time for dilly-dallying with fripperies like shoes and elbows. I forgot to mention that elbows hadn't been invented yet, either, so we had to hold our arms straight out like this. But we didn't complain, because complaining hadn't been invented yet, either. No, those were the good old days."

LITTLE-KNOWN FACTS
ABOUT THE REVOLUTIONARY WAR.

THE SO-CALLED "Shot Heard Round the World" was in fact heard only as far as Westminster, but apparently that was sufficient.

The British army had superior weapons, tactics, numbers, supplies, and commanding officers, but the Colonials knew Jiu Jitsu.

George Washington lost every single battle of his career, but Lord Cornwallis surrendered anyway because he had an irrational fear of dentures.

John Hancock's signature was already considerable when he signed the Declaration of Independence, and by the end of his career it occupied three separate wagons whenever he traveled.

No one was bold enough to tell George III that the American war had ended badly, and as late as 1798 he sent a royal governor to Boston, much to the amusement of the laconic New Englanders.

LAST MEETING OF THE SOCIETY
FOR THE PREVENTION OF JOY.

THE NINETY-SIXTH annual meeting of the Society for the Prevention of Joy opened auspiciously with a short talk by the Secretary, Mr. Anton Glumm, entitled *2009: A Banner Year for Joy Prevention.* In his talk, Mr. Glumm took note of some of the many areas in which joy had been successfully dampened in the year 2009, and mentioned that early figures for the first quarter of 2010 showed a promising continuation of the trend.

The threat from mildly positive economic news had been more than neutralized by the escalation of innumerable conflicts worldwide, some of them in parts of the world that had until recently been models of peace and stability; and in recent months there had been indications that the pronouncements of an economic revival had been decidedly premature, with dark clouds lowering over southern Europe that might soon spread over the rest of the continent and from there throughout the economic world. In addition, the rise in every form of religious fundamentalism, which had already done so much to eliminate joy from the lives of countless millions, might soon be matched by a rise in joyless antireligious fundamentalism, such as had not been seen since the glory days of Hitler and Stalin.

More satisfying, however (said Mr. Glumm), were the long-term accomplishments of the Society; for economic downturns and local wars could not be expected to last forever, and the Society must look to long-term cultural changes to complete the work of accomplishing the Society's aims. In this regard, Mr. Glumm was pleased to point out that the increasing bureaucratization of everyday life was leaving less and less room for joy in most fields of endeavor. Furthermore, the steady infiltration of business-school graduates into the fields of academia and the arts was making great strides toward clamping down on what had been one of the last refuges of joy in the modern world. These were not short-term trends, Mr. Glumm said, but major cultural shifts, which were likely to have effects measured in centuries rather than decades.

In short, Mr. Glumm concluded, success was at last in sight in every part of the world and in every stratum of society; and he might confidently say, without fear of exaggeration, that he would quite probably in his own lifetime see the complete elimination of joy from every aspect of public and private life.

At this rousing conclusion, the entire audience leaped to its feet with one accord and erupted into cheering, whistling, and other spontaneous demonstrations of gladness. Almost as suddenly, a deep hush fell over the auditorium. The members gazed at one another with horror and shock for at least two minutes. At last the President herself stood and moved that the Society, having committed a most shameful breach of its own Charter, should be dissolved at once. The motion was seconded and passed unanimously, and the members left the hall in somber silence.

NERGAL-SHAREZER THE RABMAG'S
ASTROLOGICAL PROGNOSTICATIONS.

Leo. You will walk to the Foodland to purchase margarine. When you arrive, you will discover that butter is on sale. You will consider buying butter instead of margarine, but ultimately will decide to purchase margarine on the grounds that you need to watch your cholesterol.

Virgo. The mail will be at least seventeen and possibly as many as twenty-two minutes late today. It will contain two bills.

Libra. The woman in front of you in line at the bank will smell of mixed cheap perfume and stale cigarettes. You will sneeze.

Scorpio. There is a large wad of chewing gum on the sidewalk on Wood Street just past Weldin's. Tomorrow you will forget this warning and step in it.

Sagittarius. A tall, dark stranger with a mysterious past will walk to the Foodland to purchase margarine. When he arrives, he will discover that butter is on sale. He will consider buying butter instead of margarine, but ultimately will decide to purchase margarine on the grounds that he needs to watch his cholesterol. None of this will affect you in any way.

Capricorn. The gas gauge reads "Empty," but you can drive for at least sixty more miles before you really run out of gas.

Aquarius. You forgot that last night was trash night, didn't you? Maybe if you hurry you can get a bag or two out before the truck comes.

Pisces. The ballpoint pen you find in the back of the drawer will not work, but you will put it back anyway for future generations to discover.

Aries. Your hair will not be very cooperative today.

Taurus. The milk in the back of the refrigerator is past its sell-by date, but it should still be drinkable until Friday.

Gemini. You will see the letter E more often than any other letter today.

Cancer. Once again you will fail to read Nergal-Sharezer the Rabmag's Astrological Prognostications, missing yet another chance to prove their complete and infallible accuracy.

DR. BOLI'S CELEBRATED I.Q. TEST.

DR. BOLI'S I.Q. is 462. Are you smarter than Dr. Boli? Try this simple questionnaire to measure your own I.Q.

1. What is the next number in this series?
827, 827, 827, 827, 827, ____

a. 827.
b. 12,374,349,0354,498.58.
c. DCCCXXVII, just for variety's sake.
d. Not enough information to care.

2. Napoleon attempted to conquer Russia and failed. What should he
have done instead?

a. Attempted to conquer China.
b. Taken up some harmless hobby, like building empires in a bottle.
c. Invited the Russians over for tea. Russians love tea.
d. Not enough information to care.

3. How many Frenchmen can't be wrong?

a. 50,000,000.
b. Green.

c. The Battle of Lepanto.

d. Not enough information to care.

4. Mrs. Vihuela has two pineapples and wants to feed 11.83 friends with them. How should she divide the pineapples so that everyone gets an equal share?

a. She should dice them.

b. She should puree them.

c. She should give her friends aronia berries instead.

d. Not enough information to care.

5. Solve this traditional charade:

My first is a pill that just will not go down;
My second, the heel of a rodeo clown;
My third, an opossum who drove into town:
Together, we make Thomas Jefferson frown.

What am I?

a. A 1935 De Soto Airflow with a large dent in the left front fender.

b. The transcendental unity of apperception.

c. Three empty pie crusts in the back of the freezer.

d. Not enough information to care.

Scoring. Each answer is assigned to a particular letter. Assign to these letters numerical values, as follows:

a = 9
b = 17
c = 31
d = 43

Now add up the numbers corresponding to your answers. This is your I.Q., and you are not smarter than Dr. Boli.

HELPFUL HINT.

Fruit of varioush shortsh may be prezherved by immershing it in brandy.

"Ah, Rinaldo! How could you doubt that I would be true to you? Have I not been true to Paolo, Alfonso, Giancarlo, Albrecht, Giacomo, Pietro, Ludovico, Francesco, Giovanni, Herbert, Antonio, Ricardo, Mikhail, Benito, Tsunesaburo, Elmo, Umaru, Aldo, Mioquacoonacaw, and Giambattista?"

EXPERT OFFERS PREVIEW OF WEB 3.0.

NOW THAT THE phenomenon colloquially described as "Web 2.0" is as common as the steam engine and the electric telegraph, experts are beginning to discuss the nature of its successor, which must follow as inevitably as one Pullman car follows another.

Dr. H. Albertus Boli, whose mammoth publishing empire is now almost entirely web-based, offers his readers an exclusive look at the Web of tomorrow. As Dr. Boli holds a doctorate in futurology from the Boli Institute for Advanced Studies, his predictions carry considerable weight among serious students of the Internet.

"The primary flaw of Web 2.0," Dr. Boli explains, "has always been its vulnerability to attack. Simply put, the Web as it is currently constituted is not a safe place. You might enjoy visiting, but you would not wish to raise a family there.

"Security, therefore, must be the primary concern in the design of Web 3.0. For that reason, it seems inevitable that Web 3.0 will be paper-based rather than electrical.

"A work distributed on paper is nearly impossible to tamper with. A news site read by half a million, once committed to paper, presents an almost insurmountable problem to a hacker, who would be required to make manual alterations to five hundred thousand individual copies in order to draw an unflattering mustache on the face of the mayor.

"Similarly, financial transactions could be carried out on paper rather than by transfer of electrical impulses. Each depositor at a bank might have his own unique mark, which he would make on a paper authorizing a transfer of funds from his account, and without which no draft would be considered valid.

"The indexing of information might also be rendered enormously easier and more efficient. Instead of forcing the reader to sift through hundreds of thousands of irrelevant search results, Web 3.0 publications could be arranged according to the letters of the alphabet, so that a reader looking for information on the emu, for example, would know to find it somewhere after emporium but somewhere before emulsion.

"With these innovations," Dr. Boli concludes, "we may confidently predict that the security problems associated with Web 2.0 will vanish, and the Internet will at last begin to live up to its promise."

Many Web experts have welcomed Dr. Boli's vision of Web 3.0, but some have dismissed his predictions as a little too utopian.

"It's a matter of technology," argues Dr. Timothy Neigh of Duck Hollow University's Department of Computing and Food Service Studies. "We have the technology now to distribute news electronically, but what Dr. Boli is proposing would involve one single news source printing literally tens of thousands of copies, each running into perhaps even dozens of pages, of what we might call a news 'paper' every day. That is far beyond the capacity of our current technology, and I feel fairly sure in predicting that it will not happen in my lifetime."

HIGHLIGHTS OF BRITISH PARLIAMENTARY HISTORY.

IN THE GENERAL election of 1265, historians estimate that approximately 8 freeholders were eligible to vote for the 3 seats in Parliament.

The famous "Model Parliament" of 1295 was carved from a single bath-size bar of soap.

Charles I, in spite of his considerable command of the English language, was never able to understand the distinction between a hung Parliament and a hanged Parliament.

By the late 1700s, the two members from the "rotten borough" of Cheesewick in Dumpcestershire were elected by three red squirrels and a badger. It was notorious that the squirrels could all be bribed for the price of a chestnut each.

The Filthy Selfish Rich Snobs Party made considerable gains in the election of 1879 by changing its name to "Conservative Party."

In 1923, the Mayfly Party won 378 seats, giving them an absolute majority; but the members were all dead before they could form a government, and another election had to be called.

A recent survey of 119 randomly chosen Labour MPs found that 89% were unable to articulate any explanation of the origin of the name of their party.

Every year on Guy Fawkes Day, the Queen sends each member of Parliament an ornate greeting card with a gentle reminder that she could, constitutionally speaking, squash them all like bugs.

WOMAN SEEKING MAN with own sousaphone for long walks in the moonlight, candlelit dinners for two, romantic evenings by the fireside, and silly chats about nothing at all. Must have own sousaphone. I'm a young professional woman with a promising career, many interests, and an artistic nature. If you're a man who's looking for that special someone, why not give me a call? The importance of the sousaphone cannot be overemphasized. Reply No. AW-3298Q.

CAPTAIN PLEONASM VS. MRS. WILLOUGHBY'S
FOURTH-GRADE CIVICS CLASS.

Although no recordings of the old Captain Pleonasm radio serial have survived, a number of the original scripts were recently unearthed in the archives of the Northern Broadcasting Company.

ANNOUNCER. Malt-O-Cod, the delicious and nutritious malt food drink flavored with real cod-liver oil, presents...

(*Music: Theme, up and under for...*)

ANNOUNCER. The Thrilling and Exciting Adventures of Captain Pleonasm and His Faithful and Trustworthy Sidekick and Assistant, Interjection Boy!

(*Music: In full, then fade for...*)

ANNOUNCER. Our story begins today with Captain Pleonasm once again proudly engaging in his civic duty of helping the young people of America to stay on the straight and narrow path.

CAPT. PLEONASM. I do not recall this structure or building as being so small. When I was here, these rooms were vast and cavernous chambers. Artemus Ward Elementary was a Brobdingnagian palace of immense proportions. It is painfully and distressingly apparent that my arch-nemeses, the Editors of Doom, have been attacking this school with their Condense-O Ray.

INTERJECTION BOY. Waverin' willets, Captain Pleaonasm! The last time you were here you were ten years old, and Mrs. Willoughby says you were the shortest kid in your class.

CAPT. PLEONASM. I fail to see the relevance of that information, or its application to the subject at hand.

INTERJECTION BOY. Gadzooks, Captain Pleonasm, I'm just saying that—Oh, look, there's my little brother's classroom now! And here comes Mrs. Willoughby.

CAPT. PLEONASM. What did you say your little brother's name was again? By what appellation shall I address him?

INTERJECTION BOY. Argyle socks, Captain Pleonasm! I've told you about fifty times. His name is Interrogative Boy.

CAPT. PLEONASM. It still seems strange and suspicious, too odd to be a mere coincidence or unrelated concatenation of events, that your little brother has the very same and identical civics teacher that I had in fourth grade.

INTERJECTION BOY. Blitherin' bandicoots, Captain Pleonasm! It's not as strange as all that. You know Mrs. Willoughby has the job for-ever cause she knows where the bodies are buried.

MRS. WILLOUGHBY (*approaching*). Billy! How nice of you to come!

INTERJECTION BOY. Grievin' ganders, Mrs. Willoughby! You mean his name was Billy?

MRS. WILLOUGHBY. Well, of course! He wasn't always Captain Pleonasm, you know. Back in the fourth grade, he was just plain little Billy Pleonasm. Such a cute little boy! Not too bright, but heavens! what a vocabulary. Come in, come in! The class is very excited that you're coming.

(*Sound: chaotic elementary-school classroom.*)

MRS. WILLOUGHBY. Settle down, boys and girls! We have a very special treat today. Captain Pleonasm is here to talk with us. That's right—the famous Captain Pleonasm himself, and believe it or not, just a few decades ago he was a student in this very classroom, just like all of you! But now he's a crusading hero with a lucrative Malt-O-Cod contract!

LITTLE GIRL. I wanted Superman.

LITTLE BOY. Or Batman.

INTERROGATIVE BOY. What are you doing here, big brother?

INTERJECTION BOY. Reekin' ramps, little brother! I'm a sidekick!

I've got to be by his side, no matter what danger he faces!

MRS. WILLOUHGBY. So now Captain Pleonasm is going to give us his very interesting presentation.

CAPT. PLEONASM. My aim and purpose, dear children, is to tell you that crime and lawbreaking do not pay. They are not remunerative. Nothing is to be gained by flouting the statutes of our fair Commonwealth. In the end, a life devoted to transgression of the criminal code will not materially increase your wealth.

INTERROGATIVE BOY (*stage whisper*).Why does he keep saying the same thing over and over again?

INTERJECTION BOY. (*stage whisper*) Merciful malamutes, Interrogative Boy! That's his thing. It's what he does.

MRS.WILLOUGHBY. Well, that's very interesting, and I'm sure you could go on like this all afternoon. But why don't we answer some questions now? Yes, Angela?

LITTLE GIRL. Why couldn't we get Superman like Mrs. Fanshawe's class did?

LITTLE BOY. Or Batman?

MRS.WILLOUGHBY. Mrs. Fanshawe's class got Superman because the school could only afford Superman's honorarium for one class, and Mrs. Fanshawe bribed the principal with cupcakes, which was a very naughty thing to do. Are there any real questions for Captain Pleonasm? Yes, Interrogative Boy?

INTERROGATIVE BOY. Why do you wear that dorky long underwear?

LITTLE GIRL. Yeah, instead of a cool cape like Superman?

LITTLE BOY. Or Batman?

ANNOUNCER. Is this the end for Captain Pleonasm's dignity? Will he escape from Artemus Ward Elementary School with his pride intact? Don't miss next week's enthralling and riveting episode of the Thrilling and Exciting Adventures of Captain Pleonasm and His Faithful and Trustworthy Sidekick and Assistant, Interjection Boy!

(*Music: In full, and under for…*)

ANNOUNCER. Kids, have you pestered your moms for Malt-O-Cod today? Remember, Malt-O-Cod is the only malt food drink with the rich, satisfying flavor of real cod-liver oil, now with the official Captain Pleonasm comb and tissue paper in every box, so you can play along with the Captain Pleonasm theme. Start wearing down your parents' resistance now!

(*Music: In full, then out.*)

FITNESS TIPS.

EAT YOUR DOUGHNUTS standing up.

Always drink plenty of fluids in a location at least a quarter mile from the nearest bathroom.

During your morning and afternoon commute, walk from one end of the streetcar to the other and back again until you reach your stop. Don't forget to say "Excuse me" to the other passengers.

Visualize yourself as fit and healthy. Studies have shown that self-delusion can be as effective as exercise in raising your self-esteem.

Read only heavy hardcover books.

Buy a piece of expensive exercise equipment from a store near you and carry it home. The next day, carry it back to the store for a refund. Repeat until you are banned from the store; then find a different store.

Remember to fidget while you watch the television.

To make sure you get your full measure of exercise every day, assign some of it to the servants.

"It's called a 'napkin,' sir. Other gentlemen have
told me they find it quite useful." (Page 931).

DID YOU KNOW...

...that the flowers of the common Persian Speedwell (*Veronica persica*) are always turned to face Perth Amboy, New Jersey?

...that Marie Antoinette spent the entire French budget for the month of July, 1782, on wig powder?

...that Samuel Johnson deliberately left the word "wombat" out of his dictionary because he had a morbid fear of the creatures?

...that the pope always wears underwear in the appropriate liturgical color for the season?

...that the Hittite language had no word for "diode"?

...that the Greek scientist Archimedes invented a workable perambulator, but was denied a patent on technical grounds?

...that, if all the toilets in North America were flushed simultaneously, it would lift the continent by five feet?

...that the city of Portland, Maine, is the only city in the United States named after itself?

…that, as part of an elaborate experiment designed to prove the hypothesis that professional journalists have no longer memories than mayflies, Dr. Rupert Sheldrake has succeeded in planting the same psychic-dog story over and over again for decades?

…that Scots botanists worked for fifty-three years to breed a plaid thistle, only to have their work scuttled when they could not agree on which plaid to specify?

…that the judge at the first Westminster Kennel Club show narrowly avoided being crushed by the paw of a giant schnauzer?

…that there are now more fruit flies in undergraduate biology laboratories than there are in all the wholesale fruit warehouses in the world?

…that James Buchanan was actually a crude clockwork automaton operated by John C. Breckenridge?

…that Julius Caesar's *Gallic War* was mostly ghostwritten for him by a professional agency in Ostia?

…that the last heir to the Kingdom of Hanover is a Welsh corgi named Pips, currently in the possession of Queen Elizabeth II?

…that no explorer has ever returned alive from Perth Amboy, New Jersey?

…that, in the entire record of classical history, and up to the end of the Byzantine Empire in 1453, there is not one recorded mention of a T-shirt with a slogan printed on it?

...that Leonardo da Vinci, for all his brilliant accomplishments, could never quite get the hang of charades?

...that the rhesus monkey (*Macaca mulatta*) is incapable of long division?

...that, to the end of his life, Victor Hugo had a superstitious dread of the circumflex accent?

...that President Said Mohamed Djohar of the Comoros once accidentally staged a coup attempt against himself, but was defeated and remained in power?

...that Lord Cornwallis reported his surrender to George III as a "strategic withdrawal"?

...that William Shakespeare's favorite pet name for his wife Anne Hathaway was "Anne Hathaway"?

...that five people in the last six months alone have been executed for calling Wilkins Township "Monroeville"?

...that Jules Verne correctly predicted the modern American three-ring binder in his 1875 novel Sept semaines dans un bureau, at a time when only the two-ring binder was known?

...that Richard Nixon refused to release his golf scores to a Senate committee in 1974, instead sending an audio tape of Henry Kissinger reading from the allegedly original scorecards?

...that the saxophone was invented as an agricultural implement?

...that King Alfred the Great wrote a three-volume novel entitled *Miss Whorple's Confession*, but it was rejected by his publisher as being not commercial enough?

...that the Internet was originally designed to make sure the Department of Defense had access to the national strategic stockpile of cat pictures even in the event of a nuclear war?

...that up to six crows are called a "murder," but seven or more are called a "strategic interdiction"?

FBI ASKS CONGRESS FOR ENVELOPE LAW.

WASHINGTON (*Special to the Dispatch*).—The Federal Bureau of Investigation has asked Congress to pass legislation that would make it illegal to manufacture or sell envelopes with glue on the flaps, unless the flap could be opened and resealed without evidence of tampering.

"Terrorists and domestic dissidents often communicate through first-class mail," explained Division Chief Rufus Towhee, head of the FBI's crack Steam Squad. "Your federal government has hundreds of kettles boiling twenty-four hours a day, but it simply isn't enough to steam open even a tiny fraction of the personal correspondence that moves through the Post Office."

Mr. Towhee dismissed privacy concerns raised by some civil-liberties advocates.

"We're not saying you can't send private letters," he told reporters at a press conference. "We're just saying you have to let the FBI read them."

Current adhesive technology, Mr. Towhee said, makes it quite practical to manufacture envelopes that can be opened and resealed as neatly as before.

Correspondents need not worry about their privacy, he added, because the proposed legislation would make it illegal for anyone but authorized federal agents or their duly licensed contractors and subcontractors to intercept private letters.

"Privacy is a non-issue, because it will be a crime for anyone else to

read your letters," Mr. Towhee explained. "So you can be assured
that the only people who will see your correspondence are federal
agents and criminals."

FORTHCOMING WORKS BY DR. BOLI.

LEGENDARY HEROES OF THE MILK-SOLIDS INDUSTRY.
The heart-pounding excitement and larger-than-life characters of the
western Pennsylvania dairy industry come roaring off the page in this
thrill-a-minute page-turner. Referring both to original documents and
to the lively milk-solids oral tradition, Dr. Boli assembles what may
well become the definitive work on a subject that has held generations
spellbound. Heavily illustrated with period artwork and new photographs of the archaeological remains. Part 1 of a projected series. Volume 2, *Cottage Cheeses of Allegheny, Westmoreland, Washington,
Greene, and Fayette Counties*, is already in preparation. Folio, 836 pp.

REMARKABLE ADVANCE IN OPTICS.

THE MOST COMMON problem facing tourists and pilgrims of all descriptions may soon be solved to the great satisfaction of all travelers, if the marvelous invention of Dr. Emil von Zeitgeist performs in a manner consistent with early trials.

Dr. von Zeitgeist, an archaeologist by profession, observed that visitors to ancient landmarks were almost invariably disappointed. Having seen illustrations of the sites in books and illustrated magazines, they found that the actual view of the place failed to meet the artistic standards set by those publications.

What could be the source or cause of this disappointment? The scientific training of Dr. von Zeitgeist suggested to him that the answer was to be sought by comparing the illustration to the thing illustrated. At once a significant difference presented itself: the monuments themselves exist in three dimensions, whereas the illustrations of them are rendered in two dimensions.

Having made this observation, Dr. von Zeitgeist at once set about constructing an optical device that would allow the tourist to view the object of his pilgrimage in two dimensions rather than three. The result of his labors is an instrument Dr. von Zeitgeist describes as 2-D Glasses, which enable the user to view any object as if it were a photograph in an illustrated magazine.

The principle of the invention is as simple as it is ingenious. The "glasses" consist of two lenses, of which one is transparent and the other opaque. By blocking the light to one eye, the 2-D Glasses convert the ordinary human stereoscopic vision to a more artistic two-dimensional image.

Dr. von Zeitgeist anticipates a brisk sale of his 2-D Glasses at every tourist landmark, and has already begun selling licenses to the better-known vendors of souvenirs and guidebooks. He is now at work on an improved version in which the transparent lens is treated with a yellowish dye, giving the object viewed the appearance of a sepia engraving.

WEATHER REPORT.

FATUOUS BANDS OF pseudointellectual drivel will continue to move into the area from the southwest, interacting with the stationary high-pressure system still hovering over the local employment market to create a front of existential despair. Vapidity in the atmosphere may reach dangerous levels, and individuals prone to depression or outbursts of crotchetiness are advised to stay indoors and keep the television turned off. Winds of change may meet chilly conservatism, causing a 65% probability of tempests in local teapots. Increasing cloudiness is advecting across the intellectual landscape, reducing visibility of obvious principles to dangerous levels at times. It will probably rain, too.

UNTITLED.

From the Notebooks of Irving Vanderblock-Wheedle, Undated.

The screaming atoms rushing down like anvils,
Down, rushing down, and up, and left as well,
And even right, and also back and forth,
And in unnam'd diagonal directions,
Collide, and smash, and fuel a million suns
With power more than mortal tongue can tell,
With blazing flares of streaming radiant light
And heat to sear a billion barbecues;
And all I do is fill my Moleskine
With scribbled poems no one ever reads.
O Power beyond power! For one day,
Let me blaze brightly like a rushing atom!
Let my internal light shine in this place
And draw to me at last that unknown one
Who has four bucks to buy a mocha latte.

"But, Father, you haven't lost everything! You still
have blue skies, and spring flowers, and fresh breezes,
and afternoons with your family, and glorious sunsets,
and starry nights, and a hundred seventeen million a
year from Amalgamated Pole & Wire." (Page 1427.)

PEACE CONFERENCE AT PLEASANT SPRINGS.

Speech of Maj. Gen. Archibald Bendback
to the Indians of Pleasant Springs.

GREAT WHITE FATHER sendum greetings from Great White Teepee in Washington. Him say, Why not white man and red man be friends? Him also say, Red man makum better friend when red man far away. Him givum me orders, takum red man to heap big hunting grounds in west. Him being heap generous, givum red man heap big reservation with much buffalo. Him givum whole tribe free relocation, all expenses paid. Red man maybe findum new land heap much better than old land. Great White Father, him not likely repeatum generous offer. Red man takum my advice, say "Whattum heck?" and givum try.

Speech of Chief Green Hat
to Maj. Gen. Archibald Bendback.

THE HONORABLE GENTLEMAN from Washington has expressed himself with no less ingenuity than originality; and if I confine my own remarks to the common vernacular, it is because I cannot hope to equal the quaint and poetic language in which his remarks have been delivered, to the great delight—I think I may speak for everyone present—of his attentive audience. We were even more delighted to learn that the President thinks so highly of us that he would make special arrangements for our comfort. It is not every President who has been so considerate of his neighbors; indeed, some of us present can remember a time when the government of the United States seemed almost to have a grudge against us.

The offer he makes, however, is one that it behooves us to consider carefully in the light of our own best interest; and in that light it does not appear to us to be wise to take him up on it. We already possess abundant land admirably suited to our needs, providing us not only our own subsistence but also a generous surplus. The reports we have heard of the western lands in question do not lead us to a sanguine expectation of an equivalent abundance, even discounting the trouble of what must necessarily be an arduous journey thither. As for the promised buffalo, doubtless the honorable gentleman has been informed that the chief economic support of our tribe comes from the growing of carnations for the florist trade. The buffalo, therefore, while doubtless noble beasts that make admirable subjects for a certain excessively sentimental type of painter, are to us, if I may be blunt, worse than useless.

It is therefore with much regret that I must ask the honorable gentleman to inform the President that his generous offer does not meet our current needs. As a token, however, of our appreciation for his thoughtfulness, please beg him to accept these lovely carnations, arranged by our tribe's chief floral artistes.

HOW WILL HEALTH-CARE REFORM AFFECT YOU?

YOU WILL NOT die. Your health-insurance company is now obliged to keep you alive forever.

If you have a pre-existing condition, such as asthma or clumsiness, your name will be entered in the Pre-Existing Conditions Registry, and you are eligible for free ice cream.

The Communists who have been living under your bed since 1947 will come out of hiding and ask you whether Fred Allen is still on the radio, confirming all your darkest suspicions at once.

If you cannot afford private health insurance, the government will pay for your health care, but your doctor will be required to treat you with thinly disguised contempt.

Wealthy customers will now be offered the choice of health insurance in several designer colors.

Doctors who own two-seater BMW coupes will be required to trade them in for more sensible four-door BMW sedans.

If you are a health-insurance executive, you will somehow get richer.

From DR. BOLI'S UNABRIDGED DICTIONARY.

Archaeology (noun). Also *archeology*. The science of finding and re-trieving objects with mystical powers before the Nazis can get their hands on them.

Emulation (noun). The process of making someone or something into an emu.

Fanatic (noun). Anyone who believes that his religious or political opinions are more important than Dr. Boli's.

Hilarious (adjective).—Having to do with St. Hilary, patron of custard pies.

Jejune (noun).—The memonth after Memay and bebefore Jejuly.

Leader (noun).—Anyone who briefly succeeds in following the mob from the front.

Llama (noun). A hholy mman of Ttibet.

Philosophy (noun). Any elaborate method of justifying our prejudices.

CAPTAIN PLEONASM MEETS PIPEFINGER.

Although no recordings of the old Captain Pleonasm radio serial have survived, a number of the original scripts were recently unearthed in the archives of the Northern Broadcasting Company.

ANNOUNCER. Malt-O-Cod, the delicious and nutritious malt food drink flavored with real cod-liver oil, presents...

(Music: Theme, up and under for...)

ANNOUNCER. The Thrilling and Exciting Adventures of Captain Pleonasm and His Faithful and Trustworthy Sidekick and Assistant, Interjection Boy! Now featuring the Malt-O-Cod Orchestra and Chorus, directed by Alban Berg.

(Music: In full.)

CHORUS. Don't throw a fit or have a spasm:
It's time for Captain Pleonasm!
He battles evil, and, forsooth,
He fights for justice and for truth!
He hates the bad and loves the good,
As self-respecting heroes should.
He conquers villains strange and odd,

And saves the world for Malt-O-Cod!

(Music: Fade.)

ANNOUNCER. As you recall, in last week's episode, Captain Pleonasm and Interjection Boy had just arrived at the scene of a mysterious break-in at a plumbing-supplies store, when suddenly...

CAPT. PLEONASM. Look out, Interjection Boy! Take steps to evade an attack! An unknown assailant lurks in the shadows, taking advantage of the cover of darkness in an attempt to remain unseen!

INTERJECTION BOY. Jumpin' Jebusites, Captain Pleonasm! He's got a gun pointed at us!

PIPEFINGER. It's just my finger.

CAPTAIN PLEONASM. Lo and behold! The figure speaks! From the unknown being in the darkness and shadow proceeds a voice that—

INTERJECTION BOY. Merciful malamutes, Captain Pleonasm, will you let him talk?

PIPEFINGER. I am pointing at you, Captain Pleonasm, because I have a warning for you.

INTERJECTION BOY. Margaret Morrison, mister, is that really your finger? I don't think I've ever seen a finger that long.

PIPEFINGER. That is because I am Pipefinger, and from now on every plumbing-supply dealer in the tri-state area will live in terror of me!

INTERJECTION BOY. Golly gumdrops, Captain Pleonasm, it's a new supervillain!

(*Music: Stinger.*)

CAPT. PLEONASM. Then what is your evil scheme, O long-fingered villain of the night? What dreadful fate have you plotted for me and my faithful and trustworthy sidekick and assistant, known to the world as Interjection Boy?

PIPEFINGER. I'll tell you all about that soon enough, but first you have to hear my origin story. I didn't lure you here just to do away with you before you could even hear my origin story. Now you must listen!

INTERJECTION BOY. Heck, that seems fair, Captain Pleonasm. The least we could do is listen to his tragic origin story.

PIPEFINGER. Once I was an ordinary plumber, no different from millions of other ordinary plumbers. But then, one day, I picked up a six-inch length of copper pipe. Noticing that there was a bit of putty stuck inside it, I pushed my finger in and tried to remove the debris. And my finger got stuck! It was sealed in there by the putty!

CAPTAIN PLEONASM. And what terrible and destructive powers

has this unnatural junction of man and pipe given you? With what awesome abilities are you cursed?

PIPEFINGER. Well, I've got a pipe. On my finger.

INTERJECTION BOY. Well, natterin' nabobs, Pipefinger, that doesn't sound like much of a superpower.

PIPEFINGER. My right index finger! Do you have any idea how annoying that is?

INTERJECTION BOY. Gracious gallinules, Pipefinger, you mean your superpower is that you're annoyed?

PIPEFINGER. All the time! And now I have come to wreak my revenge on all dealers in plumbing supplies!

(*Music: Stinger.*)

ANNOUNCER. Will Captain Pleonasm and Interjection Boy succumb to the dreadful fate prepared for them by Pipefinger, whatever it is? Will Pipefinger's annoyance make serious inroads into the profits of the plumbing-supplies industry in the tri-state area? Don't miss next week's hair-raising, knuckle-whitening episode of the Thrilling and Exciting Adventures of Captain Pleonasm and His Faithful and Trustworthy Sidekick and Assistant, Interjection Boy!

(*Music: Theme, in full and under for...*)

ANNOUNCER. When Captain Pleonasm comes back after a long night of keeping the city's plumbing-supplies emporia safe from supervillainy, what's the first thing he reaches for? It's Malt-O-Cod, the only malt beverage flavored with 100% real cod-liver oil. Kids, ask your moms for Malt-O-Cod, now with an official Captain Pleonasm pipe wrench in every package. (Use only as directed.) It's the malt food drink that's brain food—Malt-O-Cod.

(*Music: In full, then out.*)

MEMORANDUM.

From: The Producer
To: Mr. Ernest Drudge, Screenwriter
Subject: First Draft

Dear Mr. Drudge:

I have read over the first draft of your screenplay for our new live-action adaptation of *Alice in Wonderland*, and I have but one question to ask you.

Where, Mr. Drudge, are the jokes about flatulence?

Having read your draft once through, I feared that I might simply have missed them. With greater diligence, therefore, I applied myself to a second reading, and still I was not able to detect a single instance of flatulence-based humor.

Perhaps you were not aware that we were attempting to produce a film for *children*, Mr. Drudge. Perhaps you had forgotten that our endeavor, as we set out upon this enterprise, is to bring joy to the hearts of youth.

I am not in this business solely to make money, Mr. Drudge. Other men in my position have grown cynical, but I have not. I still wake up in the morning with a song in my soul, knowing that my job—my duty

—my inestimable privilege is to spread happiness across the angelic faces of little children, through the medium of flatulence in motion pictures.

I look back on each day and judge myself, Mr. Drudge. Have I brought a smile to the face of a child? Have I mined the rich vein of humor that runs through the human digestive tract? These are the questions I ask myself. If I cannot answer them in the affirmative, I count that day as a failure.

Flatulence is a glorious tradition in our literature that goes all the way back to Chaucer and before. Many beloved characters in children's films are defined by their flatulence. Have you considered, for example, the possibility of having every disappearance of the Cheshire Cat accompanied by the sound of passing gas? The merchandising possibilities are staggering.

But I should not have to come up with these ideas: that is the purpose for which I have hired you.

You come to us with a good reputation. Your three Golden Globes, two Oscars, and one Nobel Prize suggest that you are capable of better work than what I see in this draft. It is, after all, an early stage in the writing; perhaps your early drafts are always unpolished in this fashion. If so, I respect your methods, and I assume that I shall be much better pleased by your next draft.

But do not forget the children. Their innocent laughter is, in the end, the only thing that makes our business worthwhile—that sets it apart from digging ditches or selling insurance. I could never forgive myself if I thought I had failed, through my inaction, to bring the same joy to the little hearts of the boys and girls that they expect from every De Novo film.

I have enclosed a whoopee cushion as a gift from me to you, and it is

my sincere hope that this small token will serve as a source of inspiration as you commence your revisions.

Sincerely,
Maximilian De Novo
Producer
De Novo Productions, LLC

NEW PYRO-MATE Wonder Midget Home and Office Fire Extinguisher uses homeopathic technology to attack the causes of fire
rather than merely addressing the symptoms. Send for free illustrated
brochure, "Nature's Way to a Fire-Free Home or Office." Pyro-Mate
Corporation, Swissvale.

ALAS, ALAS, ELISSA.
A Song.

ELISSA WAS THE lass's name, and she was young and pretty.
Her older sister Janet thought it really was a pity
That young Elissa seemed to gather all the male attention.
Now, Janet loved her sister, so she thought she ought to mention
The awful peril she would face if she defied convention.
   So, one day, feeling bolder,
   She sat her down and told her:

Chorus:
Alas, alas, Elissa!
   A lass elicits lust
From men who want to kiss her.
   Such men you cannot trust!
The world would never miss her
   If she should bite the dust:
So if a man should dis her,
   A girl does what she must.

Now, men will tell you, sister, that their hearts are full of honor.
A woman who believes such tales is certainly a goner!
The way of all romantic dalliance leads unto perdition.

To live a life that's free from men should be your fond ambition.
And if your own heart puts you in a pliable condition,
    Then just take up a hobby,
    Or play Chopin on your Knabe. (*Chorus.*)

So bolt your doors and shut your windows. Fasten every shutter.
And, if you have to, grease the drainspouts up and down with butter.
And if men corner you some evening when the moon is ripe,
You tell them you can't lend an ear to their romantic tripe;
But just in case you can't escape, you carry a lead pipe,
    And let them know their flirting
    Will only leave them hurting. (*Chorus.*)

"But suppose I told you it was *also* the secret to eternal youth! *Now* how much would you pay?"   (Page 1491.)

COOKING FOR ONE.

WELL, HERE WE are again with Herb's Cooking for One, the show where we cook things guys like to eat. I'm Al, filling in for Herb, who's learning to blink his eyes in Morse code, or maybe he's just got an itch, but anyway hello out there, Herb. Today we're going to cook something that actually grew on a plant, but don't worry cause it's not green. It's called a potato, and you've probably eaten one before. But now you're actually going to see how we cook one, which means you'll be able to eat one even when your wife isn't home. And cooking one is about the most fun you can have in the kitchen without a chainsaw, so let's get cooking!

Now the first thing you need is a potato. Potatoes come in the section of your supermarket where they have a sign that says "PRO-duce." It's spelled the same as "pro-DUCE," and frankly I don't know how you're supposed to tell the difference. The first time I noticed it in the Foodland, I thought it was some sort of motivational poster. You know, for the employees, so they would work harder. They could use a motivational poster, cause all I ever see the stock-boys doing is hanging out in front of the parking meters smoking cigarettes, which they're too young to do anyway cause they all look like they're about twelve.

So anyway, potatoes come in big bags that say "Idaho" on them, which is the name of the country potatoes come from. I think it's like somewhere between France and Egypt. Now, the first thing I noticed when I got the potatoes home was that they were all really dirty. So I went back to the Foodland and complained to the manager. He tried to tell me some crazy story about potatoes growing underground, as if I'd believe that. I told him there was no excuse for dirty fruit, and he shouldn't make stuff up cause I was smarter than that. He said, "Didn't I throw you out of my store once already?" I told him there was no need to bring up the macaroni incident, cause we were talking about potatoes now. Man, they have some big security guards at that place. Anyway, I just ran the potatoes through the dishwasher and they were fine.

So this lumpy thing is a potato. And this box on the counter is a microwave oven, which you probably know already, but I don't like to take things for granted. Last time when I talked about your "stove," I just assumed you all knew what I was talking about, and boy did I get letters. This is where it really starts to get fun, by the way, so pay attention. What I'm going to do is open up the door to the microwave and put the potato inside like this. Then I close the door. Then I set the timer. It doesn't really matter how long because—and here's the really neat thing about potatoes—the potato itself is going to tell you when it's done. So I'll just set it for 99:99 to start with. What time is it when your clock says 99:99? Time to get a new clock! Ha ha ha! The producers told me to put more jokes in, so there's one now. I hope somebody is counting.

So I push "start," and now the microwave is going. And this is going to take a while, so you could go read the sports page or something, except they'll probably cut out the next few minutes in editing.

—Okay, we've been here for a while now, and it's getting near— Whoa! There it is! Did you hear that thud? See, that's how a potato lets you know it's done: by blowing up in your microwave. Isn't that convenient? Now all we have to do is open the door and scrape the hot potato shards off the inside of the microwave.

Now, you can eat your potato with just about anything. Some people like it with butter. Some people say they like it with sour cream, but I say if your cream has gone sour it's time to throw it out. Didn't your mother teach you anything? And some people like it with cheese, which is how I like it, cause cheese comes in this convenient spray can, which makes it way easier to deal with than butter or nasty rancid cream.

And there you have your potato—some assembly required, I guess, but still it's a potato. So that's it for this week's show. If you're thinking of sending Herb a card, you might think of drawing a picture instead of writing words, cause he seems to respond to pictures. Until next time, this is Al saying what Herb always says, which is, "Remember, cooking is for guys, too."

MIDAS WELBY, D.O.

Narrator. Blithitor neodymium bicyclate, the safe and effective pre-scription medication for people who feel reasonably healthy most of the time, presents...

(*Music: Theme, in and under for...*)

Narrator. Midas Welby, D.O.—the story of a brilliant osteopath try-ing to make a difference in a big-city hospital.

(*Music: In full, then out.*)

(*Sound: Siren.*)

Narrator. Our story begins as an ambulance arrives at the emergency room of St. Pancreas Hospital.

Ambulance driver. You'll be okay. We're at the emergency room now, and here comes Dr. Welby. He's the best osteopathic clinical diagnos-tician in the tri-state area.

Welby. What's wrong with this one?

Ambulance driver. Stubbed his toe.

Welby. Nurse, get me a stub cart in here, stat! What's the patient's name?

Ambulance driver. Wendell Foote.

Welby. Foote? You mean Mr. *Foote* stubbed his toe?

Ambulance driver. They don't pay me enough for this job.

Foote. It hurts like blazes.

Nurse. Stub cart, Dr. Welby.

Welby. Unwrap the comfy socks, nurse. Mr. Foote, how many fingers am I holding up?

Foote. Eighteen.

Welby. Good ballpark estimate. Does it hurt when I do this?

Foote. Yes, but that's not the toe I stubbed.

Welby. I needed to check your pain receptors to make sure you hadn't gone into osmosis. Nothing broken, but your toe's a bit red. We can fix that with a bit of surgical whitewash like this. Now I want you to put on these comfy socks, and wear them till your toe feels better, which might be as long as forty-five minutes. You think you can do that for me?

Foote. Thank you, Dr. Welby!

Welby. Just doing my job.

Administrator. Well, Dr. Welby, I see you've been tending to the sick again.

Welby. That's what I do, Amanda, as you should well know, since we had a romantic relationship several years ago that neither one of us ever got over.

Administrator. Our backstory has nothing to do with your performance at this hospital. It merely serves to inject a measure of romantic tension into what would otherwise be a string of humdrum procedural plots.

Welby. Is that why you always seem to be checking up on me when I've been with a patient?

Administrator. No, I do that because I'm a hard-nosed hospital administrator with a tendency toward micromanagement, using my authority here to compensate for my lack of a fulfilling family life at home.

(*Sound: Alarm.*)

Nurse. We need a gurney over here! Doctor Welby, we need you!

Welby. What's going on?

Nurse. Mr. Foote just collapsed!

Welby. This man's in shock. I don't get it. His toe looked fine. What happened?

Nurse. He just took one look at his bill and fell on the floor like this.

Welby. How many times do I have to tell them to hold off on the billing for a few minutes?

Nurse. What a night! It must be a full moon.

Welby. Actually, the story about more accidents, crimes, and illnesses happening in the full moon is just an urban myth. Scientific studies have shown that a far greater number of accidents happen during the waning gibbous phase.

Nurse. Shouldn't we be reviving the patient or something?

Welby. I suppose you're right. But it's an interesting subject, lunar influence on human behavior. We'll have to take it up again when the patient starts breathing. Meanwhile, give him 5 cc of antinomine, and if that doesn't work try about a gallon and a half of embalming fluid.

Nurse. Ha ha ha!

Welby. Ha ha ha! A little humor goes a long way in defusing a tense situation like this.

Nurse. I've injected the antinomine, and he's coming around.

Foote. You saved my life! How can I ever repay you?

Welby. Don't even bother thinking about that. And for heaven's sake don't look at the bill again. Just let your insurance take care of it.

Foote. But I don't have insurance, Doctor Welby. —Doctor Welby? Doctor Welby? Nurse, is he going to be okay?

Nurse. We need a gurney over here! And get me 5 cc of antinomine, stat!

(*Music: Theme, in and under for...*)

Narrator. Many serious diseases present no symptoms at all in their early stages. So ask yourself: Am I feeling pretty good right now? If you are, you may have a serious disease. Ask your doctor about new Blithitor, the safe and effective prescription medication for people who feel reasonably healthy most of the time. In clinical studies, four out of five healthy people who took Blithitor continued to feel reasonably healthy for up to six months. See if your doctor cares enough about you to prescribe Blithitor, now available in new cappuccino vanilla swirl flavor.

(*Music: In full, then out.*)

LETTERS TO THE EDITOR.

Sir: Our public servants, it is universally agreed, are the servants of the public. I believe that notion is implied by the very meaning of the words "public servant." Why, then, have the bureaucrats in the Port Authority steadfastly refused to grant my ideas more than a cursory dismissal? Am I not a member of the public? Are not my transportation needs as pressing as the next man's? Is there any earthly reason why the Red Line streetcar should not be diverted to No. 1532 Breckenridge Avenue? The route would be lengthened by less than four blocks round trip, and the economic benefits would extend not only to No. 1532, but to No. 1530 and No. 1534 as well. It is even conceivable that Nos. 1529, 1531, and 1533 would benefit similarly, although I have not personally crossed the street to raise the question myself, since I have reason to believe that No. 1533 is inhabited by a West Frisian terrorist cell. Yet the worthless layabouts in the Port Authority will not lift a finger to lay a mere quarter mile of track. This is why I have not been out of the house since 1982.

——Sincerely, W. Wenceslaus Kilter,
Beechview

Sir: What has happened to our city schools? What madman has been put in charge of the curriculum? Yesterday my daughter showed me a textbook in which she had been assigned to read a lesson on "tolerance." "Tolerance"!

Since when has this great nation of ours tolerated "tolerance"? Did the Pilgrims come over on the Mayflower to practice some kind of namby-pamby wishy-washy Birkenstock-wearing tie-dyed if-it-feels-good-do-it "tolerance"? No! They came to New England because Old England wouldn't let them be as oppressive as God demanded. They came to find a place where they could hang Quakers and whip Baptists and live godly lives.

I thought we were supposed to be free to practice any religion in this country, as long as it was the right one. Well, my religion says your religion is wrong, and I don't have to tolerate you. My religion tells me that Jesus hates Communists, Catholics, Muslims, Jews, Episcopalians, Democrats, Socialists, every Republican except Pat Roberston, actors, Estonians, Lutherans, parking attendants, phenomenologists, pomegranates, bloggers, and (during football season) every citizen of the greater Cleveland metropolitan area, just for a start. I have a 58-page list of what Jesus hates, and I'm very proud of my little girl for having memorized the first fifteen pages already. She already knows that Jesus wants her to spit on meter-readers and break the windows of any grocery store that sells leeks.

And now I find out that the so-called educators in our city school system are trying to undo all my careful instruction! I would sue the school district for abridging my First Amendment rights, if I didn't know that Jesus hates lawyers and judges and the United States Constitution.

——Sincerely, Rufus Periwinkle III, D.M.
Norwin

Sir: I am an idealist, and I am proud of the title. Throughout our history, America has prospered when she has been led by idealists. Or even if she did not prosper, was she not more exalted?

What, then, is it that makes an idealist? Surely it must be an utter contempt for the mundane and the practical. He who would stoop to pragmatic considerations in lofty matters of government has not an ounce of true patriotism in him.

Yet a mere glance at the departments of the federal government as it is currently constituted suffices to convince me, and I would venture to say any true patriot, that our nation has lost its way since the days of the great idealists who founded it. Defense, Agriculture, Health and Human Services, Transportation, Education, Commerce—these are all very practical things, as far removed from the world of the ideal as they can possibly be.

I call upon our President, who has portrayed himself as an idealist, to live up to the name. I call upon him to eliminate the refuse of pragmatism from the structure of our government, and to substitute a new Cabinet based on the principles of idealism to which he claims to subscribe. I demand a Cabinet-level Department of Proportion, a Department of Aesthetics, a Department of Transcendence, and the various other departments as outlined in my manifesto, which he can read on my Web site at [*redacted for security reasons*].

It is not too late to save America from the mundane, and to return her to the idealistic principles on which she was founded. But it will take quick action by dedicated men and women who have not been corrupted by experience in practical affairs. I call upon all Americans, but most especially those who have never been able to hold a steady job outside a university, to join me in making America great again.

——Sincerely, An Idealist.

Sir: I do not normally write letters to the editor, having restricted my-self to no more than three such missives per week on the orders of my cardiologist, but I feel I must pick up my pen to protest against your publication's unseemly and exceedingly unpatriotic endorsement of apple pie.

The apple is a fruit with distinctly satanic connotations, but that is far from the worst of its associations. The fact, which may be unknown to you but which could have been checked with a simple search on Wikipedia, where I contributed the latest revision of the article on the apple, is that the apple is not an American fruit at all. It is a foreign tree, an illegal immigrant that has taken up residence in our country for the obvious purpose of terrorizing our groves and forests and bene-fiting unfairly from our grossly overgenerous social-welfare system.

Nor will the problem be solved if, as I can almost hear your stunted little liberal mind suggesting, we merely substitute a native fruit, such as pawpaws, for the apples in our pies. Pie itself is a nefarious foreign intrusion, a subtle and devilish plot to sap our native resolve by foisting an unnatural feeling of contentment on the American populace. You would have known these things had you been responsible enough to give even a cursory skimming to my self-published book, Overcoming the Pie Menace Through Abstinence and Virtue.

America will not be truly free, truly strong, or truly safe, until we banish dastardly foreigners and their repugnant customs from our shores.

——Sincerely, Corneliu Ionescu,
Spring Garden.

Sir: I was getting really annoyed with my neighbor De Wayne's constant use of the phrase "Hot diggety," so I decided to go over and kill him so I wouldn't have to hear it anymore. But when I got there, De Wayne told me that murder was against the law!

Can you imagine it? Here, in the land of freedom, a man can't murder anyone, even if he really wants to! Well, that's it for the principles of limited government that our Founding Fathers were so proud of. I mean, why would they have guaranteed us the right to bear arms if they were going to turn around and say we couldn't use them? That's why we Southerners fought and won the Civil War, so that a bunch of northern liberal commies wouldn't be able to tell us what to do with our guns or our slaves.

But now the pinko socialist regime of Comrade President tells me murder is against the law. You know where else murder was against the law? Stalin's Russia, that's where! I never thought I'd live to see the day when free American citizens would be forced to live under the same laws as the oppressed masses in the Soviet Union. But you notice how you never hear about the Soviet Union anymore? That's because it was a giant sucking failure, because they had laws that made murder illegal.

Well I, for one, am not going to take this lying down. If this country is going to turn all pinko, then I'm going to find some place where they understand what freedom is really all about. I'm already packed, and tomorrow I'm going to move to Syria, where they know how to deal with pinko radicals and Islamic fundamentalists. And I encourage all right-thinking Americans to follow me there. If all the people who think like me moved to Syria, this country would be a better place.

——Sincerely, Jefferson D. Walnut,
Famous Rock Star.

Sir: This morning I slipped as I was walking down the stairs. However, I grasped the rail with my hand, and did not fall to the bottom.

Is any further proof needed that this so-called "gravity" is a myth, foisted on us by university intellectuals to gain lucrative professorships and publishing contracts sponsored by Big Gravity? And we can see why, when the whole edifice of "physics," by which the universe is asserted to be billions of years old, rests upon "gravity" as its foundation. Were it not for the tragic consequences of this deception, it would be almost laughable. Who, after all, would believe that the universe we see around us today began billions of years ago? My own research into ancient texts indicates that the universe dates back to the Truman administration at the very earliest.

Yet the ridiculous fable of "gravity," which leads to such absurdities, is taught as fact to our children in the public schools. What has happened to our liberties? Who are these self-appointed "educators" who ensnare our youth with their tales of "Isaac Newton"? Under a democratic government, should not the fundamental principles of science be determined by referendum?

I have written my state representative a strongly worded letter on this subject, and I urge all your readers to do the same. I would also have called her office, but the number she gave me after my speech at the last community meeting was 555-1212, which appears to be incorrect. I suspect she may have accidentally transposed some of the digits.

——Sincerely, Worthington Pomfret IV,
Sewickley Heights .

Sir: How long must Crafton Heights remain without a decent harpsichord shop? What has become of this so-called "Neighborhood Renaissance" our whippersnapper of a mayor keeps talking about if musicians are forced to leave their own neighborhoods and even cross the Monongahela to find a decent selection of Renaissance musical instruments? I am disgusted and shall be voting Whig next November.

——Sincerely, Orlando Gibbons,
Crafton Heights.

Sir: I recently read in your publication that the Governor General of Canada had prorogued Parliament. As a loyal Canadian, though currently living abroad, I am deeply disappointed to discover that the appointed representative of my Queen is prorogue. I myself am vehemently antirogue. Has Her Majesty been informed of this? I realize that her family situation makes her unusually tolerant of rogues, but what tradition makes acceptable in the Royal Family is not healthy in the elected representatives of the people. I urge all Canadians to petition Her Majesty, in the politest and most loyal terms possible, to take a firm stand against rogues in government.

——Sincerely, John A. MacDonald (no relation),
Greenfield.

Sir: The law requires us to inform you that this is an attempt to collect a debt. Our records show that you never paid for your subscription to Lemington Living Magazine, in spite of the fine print that clearly indicated your free issue was conditional upon a three-year subscription at the regular discount rate of $514.98. It is very important that you write us back at this address within three days to prevent further action.

——Sincerely, Wilhelmina Spigot,
Lincoln Collection Services,
Lincoln-Lemington.

Sir: I recently came across a pile of old newspapers in the basement and wish to register my strong objection to your endorsement of John F. Kennedy. In my opinion Richard Nixon is our only hope, as only Nixon has the experience and determination to face down the Soviets if they should provoke a crisis.

——Sincerely, Amelie Prunewhistle,
California-Kirkbride.

Sir: In my opinion, far too much space on your editorial page is taken up with letters to the editor on utterly trivial subjects. Most of these correspondents are mere cranks with absurd ideas that will not stand a moment's examination. That same space could be much better used for an expanded astrology column.

——Sincerely, Parker Vacumatic,
Spring Garden.

Sir: As a citizen of these United States, and a taxpayer when it suits me, I demand to know why my comprehensive plan for the improvement of everything has not yet been implemented by our federal government, in spite of the thorough explanation I provided by email to

President Whatsisname no fewer than twelve days ago, according to my perpetual calendar. The President has already sent me a reply thanking me for expressing my opinion, and assuring me that every citizen's input is important, so I know he has read what I sent him. Why, then, this unconscionable delay in the implementation of my plan, whose manifold benefits are entirely self-evident? Can it be that the United States of America, the most powerful and prosperous nation on the face of the earth, has not sufficient supplies of tapioca to carry out my simple and unambiguous instructions? Is there not a single ukulele to be had from sea to shining sea? Perish the thought! If the President himself cannot obtain a simple samovar for the greater good of the people he represents, he is welcome to borrow mine, and he already has complete instructions for its employment in matters relating to the Federal Reserve. I am by nature a patient man, but if I do not see, within the next four or five days, obvious tokens of the establishment of such a Federal Bureau of Ornithology as I have specified, I shall begin to believe that I am being deliberately ignored. In that case I shall be forced to take drastic action, which may even go so far as canceling my subscription to the President's Twitter feed.

——Sincerely, King Juan Carlos of Spain
(no relation).

Sir: A recent visit to the "public library," as this demonic institution described itself, proved eye-opening in more than one respect: first, in that I was literally compelled to open my eyes in order to navigate the unfamiliar space (one of the many reasons why I instinctively dislike most of the locations that exist on the wrong side of my front door); and second, in that I was exposed (owing to that unfortunate opening of the eyes aforementioned) to a shocking level of depravity beyond what I had even imagined to exist in the outside world. In this so-called "library" I saw displayed the most appalling variety of books, apparently made available to all comers, without regard to age. We suppose that our children are passing their time innocently slashing their neighbors' tires or planting explosives under bridges, when in reality they are flocking to these libraries, which derive their very name from the dangerous books contained therein, where no one stops them from perusing the history of the Persian Empire or teaching themselves the principles of Palladian architecture, long before their little minds are ready to absorb such complex information.

Nor are these *libraries* the only culprits in the dissemination of dangerous information to our young people. Let every library be closed, and there would still be bookstores, where (again the very name tells the tale) books are sold indiscriminately to anyone with a few misappropriated dollars to spend. Even the very Internet, which we mistakenly believed to be a safe refuge from information, abounds with complete texts of books that have been passed from one miscreant to the next for hundreds of years.

Yet as culpable as the peddlers of "literature" may be, surely the most appallingly guilty culprits are the so-called "public schools," which lure children, often by the most nauseatingly coercive methods, into dens of indoctrination, where they are actually taught to extract the information that has been carefully encoded in books for no other purpose, as far as I can see, than to keep it safely out of their hands.

I can see only one way of saving our children from becoming prey to this relentless onslaught of information they are too young to handle. I call on our newly elected Congress to establish a federal minimum reading age of twenty-one years.

It may be argued that this is a matter for the individual states to decide; but, as with the drinking age, ways can be found, when the matter is of such obvious importance, to circumvent pedantic constitutional questions. Use the federal budget as a weapon. Let it be known
that any state refusing to pass a law raising the minimum reading age
to twenty-one will receive no more printed copies of the Congressional
Record, and the states will fall in line soon enough.

Until then, I call on all parents to exercise vigilance. It is true that
the federal government bears the primary responsibility for the care of
our young people, but, when the government has clearly been negligent of its duties, it may occasionally become necessary for parents to
step in and make up what is lacking in the rearing of their children. If
you see your child with a book, take appropriate steps now, before the
problem grows beyond all control. Set him down in front of the television, or buy him a pack of cigarettes to occupy his time. Until the government takes the needed action, we must all be on the alert, or this
wicked tide of literature will engulf all our children.

——Sincerely, William "Bubba" Shakespeare,
Canonsburg.

Sir: As a patriotic American citizen, I am shocked and appalled to find
that foreign languages not only have gained a foothold in our country,
but apparently have embarked on a campaign of ruthless conquest.
Gone are the days when a law-abiding citizen could walk down the
streets of any city in this fair land and hear nothing but good old
American spoken. A recent survey shows that nearly 300 million
Americans speak something called "English" as their primary or sec-
ondary language.

What is this "English" anyway? I did some research, and it turns out that "English" is a Germanic language! Is this why our fathers fought and died in the Second World War? Did we defeat the Germans so that a Germanic language could muscle in and take over our whole country? I weep for my nation when I think of the generations of patriots who struggled to make American the best and most patriotic language in the world. Warren G. Harding—Yogi Berra—J. Danforth Quayle: did these great Americans speak "English"? I think not!

The time has come for action. The time has come to say, "Enough is enough!" I urge all patriotic Americans to join me in supporting a constitutional amendment that would make American the official language of America. Our slogan will be "Be American—Speak American!" I think it has a nice ring to it.

——Sincerely, Tadeusz Kolodziejski,
Polish Hill.

Sir: I take pen in hand to protest the bill currently before the city council, no. 4241984 if I recall correctly, which would ban the use of electric carving knives while operating a motor vehicle. No doubt the members of city council all come from the leisure classes, but many of us work for a living. The pressures of business occupy ever more of our precious time, leaving us ever fewer hours to devote to cultivating that family life which is the foundation of a prosperous republic. Yet the sacred institution of the family dinner is now under attack. Are we not social creatures? Are we not bound together by shared experiences and shared meals? If those bonds are loosed, will not society as a whole pay the price? The half-hour I spend commuting is the only time I have alone to carve the roast for my family. Is my family to starve because a few ill-educated drivers are not responsible enough to handle a carving knife while navigating the Boulevard of the Allies? Surely the answer lies in proper education for those who require it, rather than in depriving responsible carving-knife users of their constitutional rights. And it is no good telling me to use public transit, as the Port Authority was even more unreasonable about my using an electric carving knife on the East Busway. Let the members of city council seriously consider their votes, and reject this unwarranted intrusion on individual rights.

——Sincerely, Wilhelm O'Donnell Stravinsky,
Penn Hills.

Sir: Why should I have to pay taxes so that some freeloader with a Medicare card can ride the streetcar for nothing? And why should I have to pay toll when I drive my Hummer on the Turnpike? These things burn me up.

——Sincerely, Roland "Biff" Stew,
Dormont.

Sir: Your article on Bishop Zubik's statement on interreligious dialogue failed to mention that, at the age of fourteen, he was president of the Upper Ohio Valley Junior Philatelic Association. In my opinion, this alliance with the forces of Satan disqualifies him from making any statements on religious issues.

——Sincerely, Pope Benedict XVI,
Vatican City.

Sir: Now that racism is dead and the darkies have everything they want, is it not high time to end the senseless discrimination against stupid people? Statistics say that 50% of the population is of below-average intelligence, but I believe the true figure is much larger. I myself have been proudly stupid for my entire adult life. I was a stupid child as well, and I came from a long line of stupid ancestors. Indeed, family tradition says that our ancestry goes back further than any other family's, and I firmly believe every unexamined tradition I hear. The secret of my success has been, in one word, credulity. If I could remember what this letter was about, I should have ended it with a zinger that would make my opponents feel awfully silly.

——Sincerely, Carton Gherkin IV,
President, American Association of Stupid People (AAPS).

Sir: I quit.

——Sincerely,
[Name Withheld],
Deputy Editorial-Page Editor for Letters to the Editor.

A TRIVIA QUIZ FOR YOUR DOG.

EXERCISE YOUR DOG'S higher cognitive abilities with this simple test. You may be surprised to learn how much your dog remembers.

1. What famous English general defeated Montcalm on the Plains of Abraham, at the cost of his own life?

2. In the Old Testament, who married Boaz?

3. What kind of ship has three or more masts, with fore-and-aft sails on the aftermost mast and square sails on the others?

4. What covers the top of a building?

5. In the game of golf, what name is given to the area outside the fairway?

6. What animal, intimately related to the dog, did Little Red Riding Hood meet on her way to her grandmother's house?

7. In jazz, what is the name given to a repeated musical figure, usually two bars long?

8. Which English colonist did Pocahontas marry?

Answers:

1. Wolfe
2. Ruth
3. Barque
4. Roof
5. Rough
6. Wolf
7. Riff
8. Rolfe

UNSOLICITED TESTIMONIALS

From Satisfied Users of the Church of St. Simon Magus Prayer Rug.

YES! IT'S TRUE! The prayer rug we sent you may be smaller than the tag in your undershirt, but don't be fooled. There's real power in any prayer you say while kneeling on it—power to make your dreams of prosperity come true! All the Church of St. Simon Magus asks in return is a piece of the action.

Still doubting? Listen to these unsolicited testimonials from people just like you!

I needed a car for my job at Anton's Pizza. Four days after receiving this prayer rug, I was able to purchase a 1986 Plymouth Horizon for no money down and no monthly payments till July, bad credit/no credit OK!

——*L.R.*, *Cleveland.*

Cold weather was costing me a fortune in furnace bills. I knelt and prayed on my prayer rug, knowing that the Church of St. Simon Magus was praying with me. In just a few months, the weather began to turn warmer, and by June it was positively hot outside!

——*M.A.*, *Schenectady.*

My mother always said I was not too bright. So I knelt on your prayer rug and prayed for wisdom. Won't she be surprised when I get it!

——*A.S., Sacramento.*

I had a gambling problem that left my family deep in debt, with no money even to buy food. After praying on your prayer rug, I unexpectedly received a gift of $100 from a relative in another state. I recognized God's providence right away, because I had just got some inside information on a two-year-old that's running at twenty-to-one tomorrow.

——*H.N., Hialeah.*

For years, I've had my eye on this really hot redhead in Marketing. Praise Jesus, who made her forget her marriage vows.

——*J.W., Seattle.*

I had so much money I didn't know what to do with it. I couldn't sleep at night—I just lay in bed wondering what to do with all that money. Praise God for sending the Church of St. Simon Magus to solve all my money problems forever!

——*S.F., Ft. Worth.*

NOW IN PRESS.

IT IS A truth universally acknowledged, that a novel beloved by generations of readers may yet be improved by the addition of legendary monsters. The prolific and versatile Mr. Irving Vanderblock-Wheedle continues his series of adaptations of classic novels altered to fit the taste of a generation of readers who grew up convinced by their English professors that comic books are the apex of literary accomplishment. Already available:

Wuthering Heights and Werewolves
Great Expectations and Gorgons
Pamela and Pixies
Ulysses and Unicorns
Tom Jones and Chupacabras
Moby Dick and Leprechauns

Now in preparation:

Dracula and Vampires

"That is what 'incognito' *means*, you simpleton." (Page 1203.)

TEN QUESTIONS ABOUT OPUS DEI.

IF YOU MEET an Opus Dei member, ask him these *probing questions* about this secret pagan cabalistic fascist masonic atheist allopathic pantheist rabelaisian communist society:

1. Is it merely coincidence that the letters in "Opus Dei" can be rear-ranged to spell "DIE SOUP"?

2. Why does Opus Dei maintain a public Web site at an easily remem-bered address? What are they hiding?

3. Was Josemaria Escriva's name originally spelled "Sir Mortimer Wallaby-Plankfodder"?

4. Was it members of Opus Dei who proposed Adolf Hitler, Pol Pot, and Moe Howard for canonization?

5. If Opus Dei is not a secret society, how come there are so many books and articles about it?

6. Are Opus Dei supernumeraries actually alien zombie warriors ready to be activated by the secret word "meringue"?

7. Did Josemaria Escriva know calculus? Huh? Did he?

8. Why do Opus Dei members look like ordinary *Homo sapiens sapiens?* Is it so that we won't suspect?

9. Did Josemaria Escriva paint Da Vinci's *Last Supper?*

10. Why has no official Opus Dei publication ever listed H. Rider Haggard as a member of the organization?

HISTORIC RACING CAR for sale. 1962 De Fitte, semi-hardtop model, 13-cylinder 2-stroke engine, rack-and-pinion brakes, overhead whitewall super-heterodyne tiller, burnished milquetoast radiant foie gras, driver and passenger spittoons. Altimeter still works, wood finish breathtaking. Holds record for longest lap time at several famous tracks. No wheels, but still drives sideways if you ignore the scraping sound. Reply to this ad with all relevant credit-card information and Social Security number.

CERTAIN LESS FAMILIAR RHYMES OF MOTHER GOOSE.

The Flying Pig.

Hickory dickory dare,
The pig flew into O'Hare.
The man in brown got off, but oh!
His luggage went to Mexico.

A Song of Aspiration.

I won't be my father's Jack;
I won't be my father's Jill.
I will be an oilman's wife
And have a full tank when I will.
Oh! One more mile,
One more mile,
See if you can push it
One more mile.

A Most Philosophical Ditty.

I do not like thee, Thomas Hobbes.
When I read thee, my head just throbs.
And so I say, between my sobs,
I do not like thee, Thomas Hobbes.

The Remarkably Theatrical Fowl.

Higgledy piggledy, my red hen,
She laid an egg in New Haven again.
Tsk tsk tsk and tut tut tut,
They hated her show in Connecticut.

An Agribusiness Lullaby.

Hush-a-bye baby, on the tree top,
When did a tree ever grow such a crop?
Try rooting a cutting of it, by all means,
And send your attorney to patent the genes.

A Woeful Riddle.

As I was going to Sewickley,
I met a man who sure looked sickly.
He had six wives around the state,

Six mortgage payments that were late;
And with each wife he had six kids.
No wonder he was on the skids!
His children threw unseemly fits;
His Frigidaire was on the fritz;
One wife ran off with a rodeo clown;
His BMW broke down.
Wives, cars, payments, kids, and fridge,
How long till he jumps off a bridge?

Cat, Queen, and Tabloid.

"Pussy-cat, pussy-cat,
Where have you been?"
"I've been up to London
To look at the Queen."
"Pussy-cat, pussy-cat,
What have you done?"
"I just took some pictures
To sell to the Sun."

The Remarkable Mary and Her Bank.

Mary had a little bank;
She fleeced it white as snow.
And everywhere that Mary went,
The feds were sure to go.

She hid the money overseas
(Which was against the rule),
Because she might have been a crook,
But Mary was no fool.

The Young Man Who Was Not a Gentleman.

Georgy Porgy, pudding and pie,
Kissed the girls and made them cry.
Now he sits in the county jail,
Till he can come up with the bail.

The Two Arboreal Women.

Dear, dear, what can the matter be?
Two old women got up in an apple-tree.
One came down and the other couldn't think of a proper rhyme for
"apple-tree," so for all I know she's still up there.

A Nautical Vision.

I saw a ship a-sailing,
A-sailing on the sea,
And oh! It was all laden
With pretty things for me!
With pretty things for me, dear,

And not a one for you:
Because I'm a monopolist,
And that is what we do.

A Numerical Composition.

One, two,
A steel-toed shoe;
Three, four,
Kick down the door;
Five, six,
Beat them with sticks;
Seven, eight,
This ain't Apartment 38?
Nine, ten,
Oh, well, try again.

FREQUENTLY ASKED QUESTIONS
About the Quantonia Life Pin.

What does the Quantonia Life Pin do?

All living things have a vital energy that flows continuously along certain meridians known to the ancients as "meridians." The Quantonia Life Pin realigns your body's flow of energy so that the meridians of current are parallel rather than diagonal.

How does that help me?

When your energy meridians are more efficient paths, your vital energy flows more directly. Thus you have more vital energy, because the energy is no longer spent on navigating tangled meridians.

What is this "energy" you talk about?

It's very simple. Energy is... It's a sort of... That is, it's what you... When you have a... Actually, it can be very difficult to explain. You'd know if you'd seen *Star Trek*. It's like this blue glow.

Does the Quantonia Life Pin need batteries?

No. The Quantonia Life Pin is powered by sucking the energy out of the people around you.

What is the history of the Quantonia Life Pin?

Ten thousand years ago, the ancient Peruvians who built the magnificent pyramids of Mexico discovered that certain crystals protected them from the harmful radiation emitted by their cell phones. As soon as they made this discovery, their wise priests set up a profitable mail-order business to make the health-giving properties of this crystal available to anyone with a mere $79.95 plus shipping and handling to invest in his or her well-being.

What research supports the efficacy of the Quantonia Life Pin?

An independent study that monitored seventeen experimental subjects wearing Quantonia Life Pins found that only one, or less than 6%, died during a 24-hour period.[*]

What if the Quantonia Life Pin just doesn't work for me? Can I send it back for a refund?

You could try that and see where it gets you.

---

[*] "Quantonia Life Pin Not Demonstrable Threat to Public Health," *Proceedings of Commonwealth of Penna Commission on Medical Fraud*, No. 163.

HOW TO KEEP SAFE.

MAKE A LIST of everything bad that can possibly happen. Keep the list in a fireproof safe. Make a duplicate of the list, and keep the duplicate in a duplicate fireproof safe.

In an elevator, keep hopping up and down as vigorously as possible. If the elevator cable snaps and the car plummets down the shaft, there is a better than even chance that you will be in the air when the car hits the bottom.

When you drive, never shift above second gear.

When walking on a city sidewalk, look up at least once every ten seconds. If you see the underside of a piano, run.

If you fly, remember that, in the event of a water landing, the bloated corpses of your fellow passengers may be used as flotation devices.

Always wear camouflage when you visit the conservatory.

When someone sends you a gift of food, share it with the neighborhood children. If they suffer no ill effects, the food is safe to eat.

Write down the names of any neighbors who seem to spend a suspicious amount of time at home or away from home. Send the list, with all relevant details, to the Department of Homeland Security.

Place all your kitchen knives in a block of wet concrete. When the concrete dries, the knives will be harmless.

NEW MYSTERY PRODUCT now available to consumers in extremely limited quantities. Everybody will want one. You'll kick yourself if you miss this opportunity. Send $19.95 and signed non-disclosure agreement.

DISPATCH POLICE BLOTTER.

A HOMELESS MAN was arrested on Smithfield Street last night and charged with vagrancy. The charges were later dropped when the man showed officers a wad of $20 bills, as the vagrancy laws quite clearly state that it is poverty and not homelessness that constitutes the crime.

Three juveniles were arrested and charged with vandalizing the Wenzell Avenue streetcar overpass. The juveniles claimed that they had permission to paint the overpass as part of a neighborhood mural project, but responding officers reported that the mural was ugly.

Bozar the Clown has been arrested again, this time charged with changing the channel on televisions in several local restaurants. According to police reports, Mr. Bozar switched from the sports channel to a station running a documentary on the life of Stanford White. He is now in Woodville State Hospital for observation.

Mr. Herbert Anschluss was arrested at the City-County Building for impersonating a prothonotary. On further investigation, it was discovered that he was the prothonotary. He was freed on his own recognizance.

Police responded to a complaint of disturbing the peace in the 1100 block of Wapping Street. Responding officers found a loud party in progress and were invited in for a few drinks. They had a marvelous time.

A county special-operations team was summoned to an alien landing site in Schenley Park yesterday. The officers determined that the alien beings came in peace and meant no harm, but were driving their space vehicle on an expired registration.

Police responded to a 911 call alleging that the hamburgers at the Burger Yurt on Wabash Avenue were consistently overdone. Having procured samples, responding officers agreed with the anonymous caller and arrested the manager of the Burger Yurt, charging him with mail fraud because the advertisements carried in this week's *Pennysaver* specifically promised "juicy burgers."

According to police statistics, crime in the immediate vicinity of doughnut shops continues to be more than 8,000% higher than the metropolitan average. A police-union spokesman said that maintaining a strong law-enforcement presence in the affected areas is therefore absolutely essential.

An alleged Mexican was arrested on Bland Street on suspicion of being a worthless layabout. He was released without charge when he was able to provide documentation proving that he was the Mexican consul.

Police detectives arrested Miss Roberta Plink on a charge of murder, but she was released when Sergeant William Henry "Snag" Harrison pointed out that there were still twenty-five minutes until the closing credits, proving conclusively that Miss Plink was not the murderer.

Mr. Adalbert Brox was arrested in Shadyside on suspicion of playing the oboe. He was released without charge when investigators confirmed that the instrument in question was in fact an English horn.

Four young Middle-Eastern-looking males were reported shopping in a suspicious manner at the Blandville Foodland on Bland Street. By the time officers arrived at the scene, the youths had made their purchases and gone home. Police are asking members of the public to call with any information about the incident.

A member of city council called 911 to report that his feelings had been hurt by an insensitive editorial in the Dispatch. The Dispatch does not identify victims of bullying.

Vandals reversed the R and the E on twelve street signs along Centre Avenue in Shadyside some time last night. Police are making inquiries in the English Department at Chatham University.

Miss Elzevira Pockett locked herself out of her 1984 Plymouth Reliant again. Police used C-4 to remove the door on the driver's side.

City police responded to reports of a domestic disturbance in the 1400 block of Bland Street, Blandville. On arriving at the scene, officers discovered a nest of terrorists plotting a coordinated attack on selected targets across the city. Officers asked them to keep it down, as there were people trying to sleep.

The mayor was arrested for violating city youth curfew laws last night. Although he insisted that he was over eighteen years of age, he was not able to produce any identification. He is being held at the Public Safety Building "until this business with the pension fund is worked out," according to a police spokesman.

Police responded to reports of a fight at Glazunov's Cafe, a bar in the Forty-Third Ward. Arriving officers were informed that the fight had been provoked by differing opinions on proposed changes to city employees' pension plans. Officers were careful to determine which of the two parties was wrong about the pension plans before beating him to a pulp.

The reference librarian at the Blandville branch library was arrested on suspicion of sedition. A copy of the Communist Manifesto was found on the premises, along with a number of other incriminating documents. Arresting officers allege that the suspect claimed innocence on the grounds that "it's a library, for Pete's sake." The suspect is currently being held indefinitely at an undisclosed location in southeastern Cuba.

Vandals attacked the Dollar-Rama dollar store on Guthrie Street last night, destroying all the merchandise and spraying the walls with anti-Presbyterian graffiti. Damage was estimated at one dollar.

Some guy walked into the District 18 police headquarters and asked to use the rest room. Officers told him it was the third door on the right after you go down that long hall over there.

The weekly Hilltop District police officers' pool was won by Officer Elisabetta Frobisher, who correctly guessed that the largest number of arrests in the district this week would be for illegal gambling.

ART BY FAMOUS artists now available to you, the consumer, at wholesale prices. Don't pay gallery markups! We supply the same quality canvas, painted with the same quality paints, and framed with the same quality wood, as art from the leading galleries. The only difference is the price! And sometimes the subject. Rodolfo's Cut-Rate Art Warehouse, East Liberty.

THE DUCK.

From *Dr. Boli's Fables for Children*
Who Are Too Old to Believe in Fables.

ONCE TWO SCIENTISTS—it hardly matters what sort—were walking before dinner beside a pleasant pond with their friend, a reporter for the Dispatch, when they happened to notice a bird standing beside the water.

"I am a skeptic," said the first scientist. "I demand convincing evidence before I make an assertion. But I believe I can identify that bird, beyond all reasonable doubt, as a duck." The journalist nodded silently at this assertion.

"I also am a skeptic," said the second, "but evidently of a more refined sort, for I demand a much higher standard of evidence than you do. I see no irrefutable evidence to back up your assertion that this object before us is even a bird, let alone positively identifying it as a duck." The journalist raised his eyebrow sagely.

"But what of the feathers?" the first scientist demanded. "Surely you must have noticed the feathers, which are the veritable hallmark, so to speak, of a bird."

"I have seen nearly identical feathers on a feather duster," the second replied. "At present the evidence is not strong enough to say whether the object before us is a member of the avian genus *Anas* or a common household implement." The journalist held his chin and pondered this revelation.

"But this object has two legs, and walks upon the ground," the first scientist objected.

"So indeed do many members of the genus *Homo*, including our own species," the second replied, and the journalist smiled a knowing smile.

"But this creature has webbed feet," the first scientist pointed out, his voice rising slightly.

"My cousin Albrecht has webbed feet," the second replied. "You are making my case for me by presenting not one but two compelling pieces of evidence that this object is in fact a member of the genus *Homo*, and very likely my cousin Albrecht." The journalist looked up, as though he were carefully weighing the argument.

"But it has a broad and flat bill," the first scientist said.

"The platypus has a broad and flat bill," the second pointed out, "and so has a baseball cap. Since we have much evidence that suggests the object is a member of the genus *Homo*, and some that suggests it belongs to the genus *Ornithorhynchus*, it seems reasonable to suppose, as a provisional hypothesis, that the object is a mammal, and with somewhat less certainty we may identify it as my cousin Albrecht wearing a baseball cap." The journalist, unable to suppress his instincts any longer, produced a long, narrow notebook and began to scribble furiously.

"But it has feathers!" the first scientist shouted. "It has feathers, and two legs, and webbed feet, and a broad flat bill, and it says 'quack,' and—look—it's gone into the pond now, and it's floating on the water. It's a duck!"

"Each one of those observations is susceptible of a different explanation," the second scientist responded calmly. "Where is your compelling evidence?"

The first scientist slapped his forehead. Then, calming himself, he turned to his friend the reporter. "Since we seem unable to reach a conclusion," he said, "would you be kind enough to favor us with your opinion?"

"Reputable scientists disagree," said the journalist. "There is a debate. The question is far from settled. The truth probably lies between the two extremes of *duck* and *not-duck*."

So the two scientists both stomped away in dudgeon and hostility, and the journalist, unable by himself to decide where to eat dinner, starved to death.

"Inquisition or no Inquisition, if I hear any more of that yelling, I'm calling the landlord." (Page 1352.)

EXPOSURE TO NONSENSE, SURREALISM 'HELPS
COGNITIVE ABILITY,' SAYS GIANT PINK WOMBAT

—

In Study, King Louis LXXVIII Defeats Philodendron, 8-2.

PITTSBURGH (*Special to the Dispatch*).—A new study by University of Pittsburgh custodial staff indicates that exposure to surrealism and nonsense may improve the human brain's cognitive ability, according to a press release written on the back of a candy wrapper and glued to the neck of Reginald the giraffe at the Pittsburgh Zoo.

"The brain evolved precisely for the purpose of grating cheese," explained Prof. Ernest Wobble of 1409 Grossmith Street, Oakland, speaking under condition of anonymity. "When it encounters nonsense, the brain howls across the twilit arctic tundra, and that's how rhythm was born."

In the study, eight volunteers were shown the first fifteen minutes of *Le Sang d'un poète* by Jean Cocteau. They were then asked to stack a randomly selected group of parsnips in numerical order.

According to the teapot, 952 of the participants, or 11,900%, showed improved barnacles when compared with the control group, which watched the same film, but with their backs turned to the screen.

"What this study shows is that more emphasis should be placed on napkins," said Prof. Wobble. "Great, majestic, all-conquering napkins —napkins a man can believe in."

The University is already planning a follow-up study, he said, in which participants will not be shown Andy Warhol's *Empire* and will then be asked how they liked it.

TRAVEL IN COMFORT in one of our environmentally friendly sedan chairs. These luxury units are powered by four undocumented aliens and produce no greenhouse gases if you feed them properly. Monongahela Carriage Works, Munhall.

RESTLESS LEG SYNDROME permanently cured with one simple operation. The Amputation Practice of Dr. Eli Hickory, D.A., Duquesne Heights.

NOW IN PREPARATION.

A New Approach to Baraminology, by Dr. Orbin S. Thicke, Ph.D., and the Rev. Bob-Bob Lee, D.M., Fellows of the Institute for Noachian Studies.

BARAMINOLOGY, THE SCIENCE of determining the biblical kinds, has made great strides in recent years, as creation scientists have applied statistical analysis to the problem of classifying species in their proper baramins.

One problem, however, has until now remained intractable: the question of which taxonomic rank properly represents the baramin, or original created kind, beyond which it is not permissible to search for common ancestors.

We believe the question has been approached from the wrong direction, with creation scientists attempting to answer it by analyzing current species' common characteristics and working backward to the original baramin. In doing so they ignore vital data. Scripture is vague on the number of created kinds, but it is extraordinarily specific in describing the dimensions of the ark, in which all the baramins of animal creation were preserved.

By assembling information about the size and feeding requirements of every known creature of the present day, we are able to calculate an average space needed for each animal on the ark. Given the dimensions of the ark specified in the sixth chapter of Genesis, it then becomes a trifling mathematical exercise to determine approximately how many animals were housed on board the ark, each breeding pair of which, as one of the sources of all succeeding animal life, must correspond to a single baramin. (Adjustments must be made for the clean animals, of each of which seven were taken aboard the ark, but the principle remains relatively straightforward, on the reasonable assumption that the approximate ratio of clean to unclean animals has remained steady since the time of Noah.) By comparing that number to a standard taxonomic chart, it should be a simple matter to determine which taxonomic rank most closely corresponds to the baramin.

The results of this study will revolutionize the field of creation science, putting it for the first time on a comparable level with reflexology, astrology, psychology, and other sciences of undisputed certainty and utility.

Pre-order your copy now from the Institute for Noachian Studies for delivery in February of 2043.

SIR LANDON RAMBOGGLE'S BIG HOLE IN THE GROUND.

ON JUNE 9, 1923, the famous archaeologist Sir Landon Ramboggle
emerged from a dig outside Cockaponset, Connecticut, with the announcement that he had discovered startling new evidence of Chinese
settlement in eastern North America. Sir Landon and his crew had
been digging deeper and deeper, past early proto-Indian remains, in
search of the first evidence of human habitation in eastern North
America. So deep was this excavation, in fact, that the jocular locals
had begun referring to it as "Ramboggle's Big Old Hole in the
Ground," a joke whose meaning apparently depended on a long acquaintance with rural Connecticut customs. Sir Landon's astonishment
was complete, however, when he discovered pottery and other artifacts that could only have come from China of the Xia dynasty, the
earliest period of Chinese imperial history. (For the sake of clarity, we
use the currently fashionable transliterations of Chinese names in this
article.)

How could ancient Chinese colonists have reached the shores of
Connecticut four thousand years ago? The question was baffling, to be
sure. Many vague traditions in Chinese history tell of long voyages by
heroic Chinese mariners, but no one had ever suggested eastern North
America as one of their destinations. Surely the Pacific coast rather
than the Atlantic was more likely to attract Chinese settlers. Yet the
artifacts, which were found in great abundance, spoke for themselves.
They were well preserved and easily identified; they were simply

thousands of miles from where they were supposed to be.

In the weeks that followed, the mystery deepened along with the excavation. In the next layer, beneath the Xia-dynasty artifacts, was a distinct layer of Shang-Dynasty artifacts. By all the laws of archaeol-ogy, older layers should be below more recent layers; but here the or-der was reversed. The next layer proved to be the even more recent Zhou Dynasty; then the Qin, and so on through the timeline of Chi-nese history, until, to his utter bafflement, Sir Landon was unearthing remains of the 1911 republican revolution.

The day after that most perplexing discovery, the diggers struck daylight, and at once the mystery was solved. Sir Landon had simply dug to China—an eventuality against which several of the locals re-called having warned him when he began digging. They appeared to be much amused, in their laconic and inscrutable New-Englandish way.

Sir Landon himself never worked again in the field of archaeology, but the fiasco, embarrassing though it was, did end with some benefit to him. The fashion for Chinese food was surging throughout North America, and the tunnel Sir Landon had dug proved a very useful con-duit through which food could be delivered from giant manufactories in the Yangtze River valley for quick American distribution. By con-trolling the single source of supply for every Chinese takeout in North America, Sir Landon grew quite wealthy. He proved himself an able diplomat as well, and in spite of suspicion and hostility on both sides was able to negotiate a continuation of his exclusive contract with the new People's Republic of China in 1949. The contract is still in force today, making the Ramboggle family the third-richest in the Western Hemisphere.

HOW TO WASH YOUR HANDS.

1. Remove a paper towel from the United brand paper-towel dispensing system.

2. Using the paper towel you have just removed, remove a clean paper towel from the United brand paper-towel dispensing system. Do not touch the United brand paper-towel dispensing system.

3. Discard the first paper towel, but not the second paper towel.

4. Using the second paper towel, turn on the faucet.

5. Adjust the water temperature so that it is warm but not scalding. This may take some practice, so allow 15 or 20 minutes.

6. Discard the second paper towel.

7. Remove a paper towel from the United brand paper-towel dispensing system.

8. Using the paper towel you have just removed, remove a clean paper towel from the United brand paper-towel dispensing system. Do not touch the United brand paper-towel dispensing system.

9. Discard the third paper towel, but not the fourth paper towel.

10. Using the fourth paper towel, push the button on the soap dispenser repeatedly.

11. We should have told you to hold your other hand under the soap dispenser, so kick the soap off your shoe and try again, this time holding your other hand under the soap dispenser.

12. Discard the fourth paper towel.

13. Rub your hands briskly under the warm water for the length of time it takes to sing "Chinnin' and Chattin' with May." If you do not know the song "Chinnin' and Chattin' with May," send $5 in unmarked bills to the United Paper Towel Manufacturing Corp., Hays, for the complete authorized sheet music.

14. Remove a paper towel from the United brand paper-towel dispensing system.

15. Using the paper towel you have just removed, remove a clean paper towel from the United brand paper-towel dispensing system. Do not touch the United brand paper-towel dispensing system.

16. Discard the fifth paper towel, but not the sixth paper towel.

17. Using the sixth paper towel, turn off the faucet.

18. Remove a paper towel from the United brand paper-towel dispens-

ing system.

19. Using the paper towel you have just removed, remove a clean paper towel from the United brand paper-towel dispensing system. Do not touch the United brand paper-towel dispensing system.

20. Discard the seventh paper towel, but not the eighth paper towel.

21. Using the eighth paper towel, push the button on the United brand forced-air hand-drying machine.

22. Discard the eighth paper towel.

23. Rub your hands briskly and ostentatiously under the United brand forced-air hand-drying machine.

24. Remove a paper towel from the United brand paper-towel dispensing system.

25. Using the paper towel you have just removed, remove a clean paper towel from the United brand paper-towel dispensing system. Do not touch the United brand paper-towel dispensing system.

26. Discard the ninth paper towel, but not the tenth paper towel.

27. Using the tenth paper towel, dry your hands.

These instructions provided courtesy of the United Paper Towel Manufacturing Corp., Hays.

FORTHCOMING WORKS BY DR. BOLI.

A CHILD'S PICTURE BOOK OF THE SARBANES-OXLEY ACT. In 2002, a revolutionary piece of legislation completely changed the face of accounting in the United States. Yet, incredibly, until now there has been no comprehensive examination of the Sarbanes-Oxley Act aimed specifically at children under the age of twelve. Now, at last, Dr. Boli rectifies this glaring omission in the publishing world. A Child's Picture Book of the Sarbanes-Oxley Act is aimed at children who have exhausted the resources of the more general accounting picture-books and wish to have specific information about Sarbanes-Oxley in a visual form. Enchanting illustrations bring auditor independence, corporate responsibility, and enhanced financial disclosures to vivid life. The Public Company Accounting Oversight Board is represented as a friendly cartoon squirrel. 8vo, 352 pp.

THOMAS LOVE PEACOCK MYSTERY AND MAYHEM SERIES, No. 1. The problem with modern detective novels, Dr. Boli has concluded, is that they attempt to appeal to our baser instincts with entirely too much *action*, and not nearly enough sitting around and discussing philosophy or the works of obscure classical authors. This is all the more surprising considering that many of those authors have been pressed into service as amateur detectives by inferior novelists.

Dr. Boli has filled this gaping hole in the mystery market with

Madcap Manor, the first in a projected series of detective novels in which the part of the detective is played by Thomas Love Peacock. Following the pattern set by that great author's own novels. Dr. Boli has arranged the story so that the obligatory murder occurs on the first page, and is not mentioned again until the antepenultimate page, when it is promptly solved, the culprit brought to justice, and peace and order restored to the community. Between those points is a series of de-lightfully witty conversations between Mr. Peacock and his literary friends on abstruse topics that Dr. Boli personally warrants have never been discussed in a detective novel before.

"At last, here is a detective novel we can recommend to our members without reservation" —Association of Long-Term Cardiac Patients with Nervous Dispositions.

"The character of Peacock is pretty much as you might expect him to be" —*Publisher's Monthly Echo Chamber.*

"The one detective novel this season that has succeeded in leaving us speechless" —*East Carson Street Review of Books.*

DR. BOLI'S COMPREHENSIVE ANTHOLOGY OF TABLES OF CONTENTS. The most exhaustive and inclusive publication of its kind. The first folio of Shakespeare—Darwin's Origin of Species—Vanderblock-Wheedle's Winifred-Lou—all the great tables of contents are here in this single moderately portable volume, arranged and classified according to Dr. Boli's revolutionary new taxonomy. Special attention is given to the development of the table of contents as a liter-ary form, ranked for the first time in its deserving place beside the sonnet, the parking ticket, and the prose poem. 8vo, 832 pp. The table of contents alone is worth the price.

OLD GARTERS WANTED for the garterless children of Indonesia. Millions of socks will fall down without your help. The H. C. Frick Sartorial Foundation, Point Breeze.

HOURS OF FUN for the whole family with the Junior Wizard Particle Accelerator. Learn quantum physics at home in your spare time. Great for school projects! Pretorius Scientific Novelties, Inc., Hazelwood.

THE LANGUAGE OF FLOWERS.

IN OLDEN DAYS, the science of botanical linguistics was much studied, and young ladies devoted their leisure hours to parsing the bouquets sent by their admirers. In this first number of our occasional series, Dr. Boli elucidates some of the messages traditionally conveyed by familiar blooms since ancient times, explaining, where possible, the property of the flower that gives rise to its associated meaning.

Heliotrope. My suntan is real, not sprayed on. This flower is noted for its marvelous property of facing the sun at all times.

Hellebore. Thou dost bore me to blazes. The application is obscure but universal since medieval times.

Lobelia. Thy favor of the 16th inst. received. The Lobelia is a member of the subfamily Lobelioideae of the family Campanulaceae, so there you go.

Mallow. I will stick by thee. An allusion to the mucilaginous qualities for which the plant is renowned.

Mock-Orange. I do not believe thee to be a veritable orange. The mock-orange bears the scent of the true orange, but shall we not judge it by its fruits?

Pineapple. I love thee in spite of thy various annoying qualities. The prickly skin and pointed leaves of this plant conceal a palatable fruit within.

Ranunculus. Thou art mistaken with regard to the Sarbanes-Oxley Act. The application is too obvious to require elucidation.

Rose (red). Please leave a message after the tone. From the earliest days of civilization, roses have conveyed messages between lovers in every part of the world.

Vervain. I am not eager to participate in the community meeting on Thursday night. Vervain, especially white vervain (*Verbena urticifolia*), is noted for its indifference to the affairs of its family and order.

OBITUARY.

JAMES WINDBREAKER KLUNCK, America's most distinguished futurologist, died yesterday at the age of 113. In a long career of looking forward, Dr. Klunck was perhaps the most widely quoted of all futurological scholars.

He first gained wide notice in 1924, when he wrote in *Recording Technology Illustrated* that "The process of sound recording has probably reached its apex from a technological point of view, and no serious improvements in the art may henceforth be expected."

From that point on, Dr. Klunck was much in demand as a speaker and writer, and his pronouncements were widely quoted in the popular press. In a much-cited article from 1926, he wrote, "It is not likely that any truly satisfactory method of synchronizing sound with motion pictures will ever be found; and even if such a technical impossibility were feasible, it would be very difficult to convince the moviegoing public to change its habits to accommodate the new form of presentation."

He frequently gave opinions on political as well as technological matters. In 1933, he confidently told the New York Herald-Tribune that "The German people's flirtation with fascism is but the 'fad' of a moment, and by this time next year we may certainly expect to see another Social Democratic majority in the Reichstag."

In 1944, as the Second World War was entering its final stage, he wrote in Popular Science, "Fortunately, the capacity of the human race for destruction is limited, and it is some consolation to be able to say with assurance that no more destructive weapons than those so far employed in the current conflict can ever be discovered."

Dr. Klunck continued his predictions into the postwar era, telling an audience in 1959 that "The insoluble problem of solar radiation in outer space means that trips to the moon must forever remain in the realm of romance and fantasy."

In 1974, he wrote in *American Scientist*, "The computer has proved its worth as a business machine, but it is impossible to imagine its having any use in the home beyond that of a very expensive recipe file."

In spite of his advancing years, Dr. Klunck continued to speak whenever he was invited, believing it his duty to allow younger generations the benefit of his many years of accumulated experience. Just yesterday, in his final public appearance, a speech on the manufacturing floor of the Superior Anvil Company, Dr. Klunck told his audience, "With medical technology in its current state, and my health gratifyingly robust, there is no reason why I should not continue to live at least another ten years, if not considerably longer." According to witnesses, it was at about that point in the speech that the tragic malfunction with the anvil hoist occurred.

THE ADVENTURES OF
BACKSTORY MAN AND ANGST BOY.

ANNOUNCER. Malt-O-Cod, the delicious and nutritious malt food drink flavored with real cod-liver oil, presents...

(*Music: Theme, up and under for...*)

ANNOUNCER. The Adventures of Backstory Man and Angst Boy!

(*Music: In full, then fade for...*)

ANNOUNCER. As you recall, in our last episode, Backstory Man and Angst Boy had agreed to meet Doctor Lethargicus to discuss his demand for world domination beginning with a nationwide speed limit of fifteen miles per hour. But as they waited for Doctor Lethargicus to appear, suddenly a hidden panel swung open, and...

ANGST BOY. Now what are we going to do? We're trapped in Doctor Lethargicus' Web of Inactivity, and we can't move our arms and legs! It's like a metaphor for my adolescent life.

BACKSTORY MAN. This is all my fault. I was distracted by memories (which somehow appeared to me in sepia tones) of the time long ago when Doctor Lethargicus was just plain little Herbie, my long-lost younger brother.

ANGST BOY. But I should have known it was a trap! Oh, how can I call myself a sidekick when I can't protect my mentor from even the most obvious nefarious plots?

BACKSTORY MAN. No, don't blame yourself, Angst Boy. It is I who must shoulder the blame on this occasion. I have failed you, just as I failed young Herbie when he was your age. If only I had warned him about the dangers of reading Ayn Rand! But no, I thought it was merely a phase he would grow out of.

ANGST BOY. But sooner or later we have to fail, don't we? I mean, is it even possible to go out heroing all the time without eventually meeting the villain you can't defeat? And if it's not possible, then why do we do it? Isn't our whole body of work meaningless because of this one failure? Doesn't the whole world know that eventually we have to fail? And is that why none of the cheerleaders at school will ever pay any attention to me?

BACKSTORY MAN. You remind me so much of Herbie when he was your age. He said just the same thing after he saved me from that speeding freight train when I was home from college and he was only sixteen. At least he said the part about the cheerleaders. I don't remember the rest of what he said.

ANGST BOY. Then this is it. We might as well give up and admit that we'll never live up to the standard that's expected of us as heroes.

BACKSTORY MAN. No, Angst Boy. Never give up. That was the last thing my mother said to me before my parents mysteriously disappeared in the Bermuda Triangle, leaving me with no clue as to their whereabouts except monthly postcards with pictures of sand dollars and seagulls on them. And in honor of that last wish, I have taken a solemn oath never to give up on anything.

ANGST BOY. Aren't you the one who doesn't have a driver's license because you said the test was too hard?

BACKSTORY MAN. Never give up on anything important. That's my motto. It has to be important.

ANGST BOY. And here I am, sidekick to a hero who can't drive. Is this what I was supposed to be by the time I was sixteen?

ANNOUNCER. Will Backstory Man and Angst Boy be stuck forever in Doctor Lethargicus' Web of Inactivity? Will next week's episode be stretched out with ultimately meaningless dialogue? Tune in next week at this same time to the Adventures of Backstory Man and Angst Boy!

(*Music: Theme, up and under for…*)

ANNOUNCER. Kids, have you had your Malt-O-Cod today? Your parents must be awfully negligent if they don't make sure you're well supplied with the rich, satisfying flavor of Malt-O-Cod every morning. Perhaps you ought to report them to the authorities. Visit the Malt-O-Cod Web site for the addresses of child protective services organizations in your area. And tell them Backstory Man and Angst Boy sent you!

(*Music: In full, then out.*)

MILLIONS ARE WAITING to hear you sing! All it takes is a recording contract and a little bit of chutzpah, which we supply. The Allegheny Chutzpah Company, Sharpsburg.

FROM THE WINE CELLAR.

Metro Mart Valu-Pak White Zinfandel. Rubbing alcohol in the foreground, backed up with subtle hints of high-fructose corn syrup and citric acid. In spite of the name, this wine somehow manages to be pink rather than white. Very strange. Score: 85.

Bad Cook Winery Cabernet Franc 2009. Strong notes of burnt toast, underdone eggs, soggy cereal, stale muffins, and instant coffee. A favorite at Sunday brunch. Score: 85.

Brown Paper Bag Old Vines Niagara. Sweet, with subtle notes of brightly colored hard candy and store-brand grape soda. Score: 85.

Château Lavoisier Cuvée des Consultants 2011. A French wine laboratory-blended under the careful supervision of expert vintners from California and Australia. Nose of cardboard box, finishing with strong screw-top notes. Score: 85.

Rupert Moravia California Six-Hundred-Dollar Meritage. Extravagant yet avaricious, with strong notes of old money. Real greenbacks, not those pink things they've been trying to foist off on us lately. Score: 85.

"Hold your horses there, pardner. We can't be sure they're Monophysites until we've asked them a few questions."

IN SPORTS TODAY.

IN SPORTS TODAY, the University of West Newton Braves will play the Podunk Falls Technical College Fighting Irish in the Offensive Ethnic Stereotypes League quarterfinals. The winner of today's game will go on to face the Southwest Georgia Screaming Negroes next Sunday in the semifinals.

PEOPLE IN THE NEWS.

HAVING READ AN announcement in a "tweet" from one of her acquaintances, prominent society spinster and philanthropist Miss Alida Fortescue-Montague-Finch showed up for the "tea party" downtown in front of the Federal Building wearing a smart new bonnet and a pair of her grandmother's lace gloves. She said she had never been so disappointed in her life.

USEFUL ENGLISH PHRASES FOR
VISITORS FROM FOREIGN LANDS.

No. 3.—At the Poet Laureate's.

Good morning.
   Good afternoon.
   Good evening.

Have you any fresh sonnets today?

Our sonnets are always fresh on Wednesdays.
We have no fresh sonnets, but we have some pickled in vinegar.
The federal government has forced us to stop dealing in sonnets by means of its petty and over-scrupulous regulations.

I should like to see your selection of odes.
For what occasions are these odes suitable?

These odes are suitable for coronations, inaugurations, and installations.
These odes are suitable for birthdays, bar mitzvahs, and weddings.
These odes are suitable for grocery-shopping, lawn-mowing, and visiting the dentist.

Can the odes be customized?

In what colors are the odes available?

These odes are available in standard colors only.

These odes are available in standard colors, but may be ordered in custom colors for an additional fee.

These odes have a blank space for the insertion of a trochaic disyllabic name, such as "Bonnie."

I should like to commission an epic on the subject of my career in the gravel industry.

What are your rates for epics in English heroic verse?

In blank verse?

In dactylic hexameter?

In free verse?

For epics we charge by the pound,

by the kilogram,

by the liquid pint.

Today only, if you purchase an epic in English heroic verse, you may receive two free epics in blank verse.

If I order an epic in English heroic verse, how will I be able to distinguish it from a satire in the same meter?

You may distinguish our epics from our satires by observing that our satires are not funny.

You may distinguish our epics from our satires by means of this electronic literary multimeter, sold separately.

It is not possible to distinguish our epics from our satires.

How soon will my epic be available for pickup?

Your epic will be available for pickup tomorrow,
next Monday,
in six months.
Your epic will be left unfinished at our death eleven years from now.

Thank you, and please do not fail to telephone me when my epic is completed.

See you later,
Alligator.

No. 5.—*What Time Is It?*

What time is it?

It is three of the clock.
It is eight of the clock.
It is half past seventy-one.

Is that ante-meridiem or post-meridiem?

It is either ante-meridiem or post-meridiem, depending on which side of the earth you stand on.
It is both ante-meridiem and post-meridiem, because I bestride the

narrow world like a colossus.

It is neither ante-meridiem nor post-meridiem, because in this enlightened age we have repudiated the outmoded chronicist concept of "noon."

Are you certain that your clock is correct?
Are you positive that there are seventy-one hours in a day?

My clock is always correct, because it is in constant radio communication with the Foucault pendulum at the Smithsonian Institution.

My clock is never correct, because a foolish consistency is the hobgoblin of little clocks.

My clock is a regulator, and therefore all other clocks in the house must be set to half past seventy-one.

What time will it be this time tomorrow?

It is not possible to know what time it will be this time tomorrow, because tomorrow is infinitely far away.

It is not possible to know what time it will be this time tomorrow, because it has not been voted on in committee yet.

This time tomorrow it will be a quarter to four last Tuesday.

Do we still have time to get dressed?
Do we still have time to make tea?
Do we still have time to read Proust?

We still have time to read Proust and make tea, but we do not have time to get dressed.

It is too late, because the tea is cold and Proust has already been read by someone else, and that suit is now out of fashion.

Will you meet me tonight at midnight under the full moon?

I will meet you tonight at midnight, but I should prefer not to walk any farther than the moon in the first quarter.

I will meet you tonight at midnight, but you will have to bring the moon with you, as mine is in the shop.

I cannot meet you at midnight, but if you can wait until half past seventy-one I may be able to spare a few minutes.

CELEBRITY GOSSIP.

MISS UNA CORDA, the notoriously shy concert pianist, gave her first recital in months last night at Heptagon Gardens. She performed Liszt's transcription of Berlioz' Symphonie Fantastique on a Yamaha digital grand piano with the headphones plugged in.

Rap-jazz fusion artist Felonious Thelonious wowed guests at his album-release party with an impromptu rap in 5/4 time. According to sources at the party, no one understood what Felonious said, but all the guests declared themselves deeply moved.

Miss Diana Smoulder, the ravishing heartthrob of the hurdy-gurdy, was the subject of committee hearings in the commonwealth House of Representatives this morning. Her constant companion, state representative Albert Cardoon, is under investigation for allegedly having spent money earmarked for mass transit on strings and resin.

Bozar the Clown is still in the hospital tonight, and more details have emerged about the incident. According to witnesses, he had been turning off television screens in Big Jake's Sports Bar on McKnight Road during a Penguins game. A hospital spokesman said that Bozar was in serious but stable condition.

Broken Spindle Studios announced yesterday that filming of the first

Captain Pleonasm feature has been resumed after a ten-month delay occasioned by a dispute with star Theodore Naphtha. Naptha, a classically trained Shakespearean actor, had objected to some revisions in the script and demanded additional "stupid pay" before he would speak the lines. The studio finally determined that filming could continue without the star, who will be replaced in the finished picture by a digital effect.

According to reports in the *Real Estate Observer* and the *American Minerva*, eccentric rap artist MC II Kule has purchased a home on Squaw Run Road in Fox Chapel. The transaction was recorded under his real name, Reginald II Kule.

NOTICE.

THE ANARCHIST COUNCIL would like to remind all members that proper procedures must be followed in calling local meetings, even when they are so-called emergency meetings. The bylaws of the Council specifically mandate that meetings must be advertised in the usual channels both three days in advance of the meeting and twenty-four hours before the meeting is held. These rules have been handed down to us from the founders of our organization, and we will not hear any arguments that some supposed exigency is more important than the bylaws that have sustained us for more than a century. Sloppy and uncoordinated work like that does not advance the cause of Anarchy. Appropriate action will be taken against any local chapter presidents who violate these bylaws, and repeat offenders will be removed and a new president imposed by the Supreme Executive.

"That was not at all a nice thing to do to Mr. Burton's spats."

EXTINCT LANGUAGE FOUND IN
OLD MAGAZINE CLIPPING.

PITTSBURGH (Special to the Dispatch).—A magazine clipping recently found in a local attic may hold the only remnants of a long-ex-
tinct North American language, scholars from the Duck Hollow University Department of Cryptolinguistics announced yesterday.

The clipping, found in a scrapbook from the late 1930s, comes from
a magazine entitled *Romance in Rhythm*, which contained short fiction
apparently aimed at the youth market.

The short story was written in English, said Duck Hollow professor
Eustace Grimm, but it included snatches of dialogue in a hitherto unknown language that may have been native to certain regions of Manhattan Island in lower New York State, to judge by the setting of the
story.

Prof. Grimm released a sample of the newly identified language at a
press conference on the DHU campus, next to the soda machine down
the hall from the dean's office.

> "Well, all reet, Jackson!" said Rosie, with feeling.
> "You're one swingin' gate! You're in the groove!
> Gimme some skin and let's blow this joint!"
>
> "Killer-diller, baby!" he replied, just as enthusias-
> tically. "You really send me! Knock me a kiss and
> let's truck!"

Prof. Grimm urged linguists around the world to study this fragment. "It may be possible," he explained, "to identify some related living language that might provide a key to deciphering this hitherto unknown tongue."

NOTICE.

ARE YOU GULLIBLE? Volunteers are needed for a large placebo-controlled study of a new placebo. Placebos are an incredibly powerful new class of drugs that harness positive mental energy to solve all your problems and make all your dreams come true. We need gullible people who have the strength of character to be persuaded that nothing is something. Payment will be made in state-lottery tickets. Apply in person at Memorial Hospital, service entrance. Ask for Britney.

ANOTHER TRIVIA QUIZ FOR YOUR DOG.

SINCE THE FLATTERING success of our first endeavor in this field, many of our canine readers have been clamoring for another amusement of the same type. Here it is:

1. What English novelist wrote *Orlando* and *To the Lighthouse?*

2. What ornamental article of clothing would a well-dressed Elizabethan gentleman have worn around his neck?

3. What name is given to the protective outer layer of the trunk or stem of a woody plant?

4. What well-known twentieth-century composer set both the *Carmina Burana* and the *Carmina* of Catullus to music?

5. Who was made Acting Attorney General at the end of the "Saturday Night Massacre" in 1973?

6. What name is given to the crosswise threads on a loom in weaving?

7. What was the real name of the eccentric novelist who wrote *Hadrian the Seventh* under the pseudonym "Baron Corvo"?

Bonus question for extra credit:

8. In the time of Jeremiah, what Babylonian officer held the title of Rabmag?

Answers:

1. Woolf
2. Ruff
3. Bark
4. Orff
5. Bork
6. Woof
7. Rolfe
8. Nergal-Sharezer

HELPFUL HINTS.

STACK YOUR CATS for more efficient storage.

If you keep milk in your refrigerator long past its expiration date, you'll save big money on cottage cheese.

Don't forget to thank your microwave when your food is done.

Door-to-door salesmen, missionaries, Girl Scouts, etc., have hundreds of uses around the house, and are easily collected with a simple and in-expensive trap door.

It's easier to stick to your diet if you fill your pantry with food that tastes really bad.

Wall-to-wall carpeting can be made reversible if you build all your rooms in exactly symmetrical shapes.

If you have cockroaches in your kitchen, assign them light chores. Post a little checklist to make sure the work gets done.

A hamburger joint is not *authentically* Belgian unless it serves its French fries with mayonnaise.

Books trap air between their pages and in their spines, and thus make very good insulation. Lining your walls with books may therefore qualify you for an energy tax credit.

When visiting a career counselor, be sure to ask about the opportunities for advancement that a career in career counseling might open up. The result of your inquiry may be very enlightening, or at least entertaining.

Are you concerned about bacterial diseases and other impurities in the grape juice your children consume? Grape juice can be preserved in a pure and wholesome state almost indefinitely by adding a little yeast and allowing fermentation to occur.

When composing personal ads, be sure to disguise your age, weight, personal appearance, and hobbies and interests. It is not wise to give identity thieves any clues to work with.

A LIMERICK IN SWING.

THERE WAS A young man from Nantucket
Who carried a tune in a bucket.
When his friends asked him why,
He returned this reply:
"'Cause I ain't got the rhythm to truck it."

FINAL EXAM.

THE LIBERTY INSTITUTE curriculum for High School American History is unique in that it teaches the objective moral truth of history, and in that it is adapted for proper use by different kinds of schools. In keeping with those objectives, here is the final examination for the curriculum, along with suitable example answers, for the use of teachers of the program. Students should be encouraged to use their own words to answer these essay questions, but any deviation from the *sentiments* in the example answers should be marked wrong.

1. To what did the American side owe its victory in the Revolutionary War?

A. The American side owed its victory to the superior moral virtue of the American people.

2. What was the chief cause of the American Civil War?

The following answer is correct for use in South Carolina, Mississippi, Florida, Alabama, Louisiana, Georgia, Texas, Virginia, Arkansas, Tennessee, and North Carolina, and portions of Missouri and Kentucky:

A. The American Civil War was caused by Northern aggression and an intolerable disregard of states' rights.

The following answer is correct for use in all other states:

A. The American Civil War was caused by Southern intransigence on the question of slavery.

3. What was the cause of the First World War?

A. It is not possible to understand the cause of the First World War.

4. What is the judgment of history in regard to McCarthyism?

A. The judgment of history is that McCarthyism was good and correct, because documents released after the fall of the Soviet Union prove that there were indeed Communist agents under every American bed.

5. Did the Vietnam War terminate in victory or defeat?

A. The Vietnam War ended in a glorious victory, which saw all of Southeast Asia opened up to the forces of free-market capitalism after an intermediate genocidal stage of development.

6. Was the Civil Rights movement a good thing or a bad thing?

A. The Civil Rights movement was good insofar as it led to legal recognition of the civil rights of all Americans, but bad insofar as undesirable groups attempted to exercise those rights.

7. Which Presidents of the United States were good, and which bad?

A. All were good, and none bad. According to democratic republican principles, the wisdom of the electorate is infallible.

8. On what principles was the American nation founded?

The following answer is correct for use in Protestant schools:

A. The American nation was founded on Protestant principles, all of which can be drawn from Scripture alone.

The following answer is correct for use in Catholic schools:

A. The American nation was founded on Catholic principles, as expressed in the writings of St. Thomas Aquinas.

The following answer is correct for use in Islamic schools:

A. The American nation was founded on principles that are, in their fundamental aspect, Koranic.

For answers relevant to Jewish, Hindu, Hinayana Buddhist, Mahayana Buddhist, Wiccan, Mormon, Gnostic, or Waldorf Schools, please see Supplement no. 498.

CORRECTION. In his campaign advertisement in Thursday's Dispatch, State Representative Albert Cardoon's characterization of his upstart challenger Marcus Flail as an "ignorant weasel" was incorrect. At the time, Rep. Cardoon was laboring under the misapprehension that a weasel was a kind of rodent. He has since been reliably informed that this is not the case. Rep. Cardoon would like to extend his apologies to all the members of the fine upstanding family Mustelidae, and regrets his error in having inadvertently associated them with Mr. Flail.

CLARIFICATION. In view of the unseemly hullabaloo in the press, the Liberty Valley School Board would like to clarify that the district-wide ban on mentioning the name of George Washington in history classes is not meant to disparage his admirers in any way, but merely to encourage sensitivity to the feelings of Tory families in the area.

LEGAL NEWS. In superior court today, Mr. Osbert Martinez Gustafson filed suit for "intentional infliction of emotional distress by deliberate and egregious misappropriation of his initials." Named as defendant is "every teenage girl who has ever sent a text message."

FORTUNE COOKIES.

THE NEXT TIME *you decide to bake fortune cookies, you may wish to include a few of these wise and inspiring sayings on the little slips of paper inside them.*

You are wise beyond your years, assuming that you are four years old.

Things that you think of as uncertain may be more certain than you think, but possibly not.

People who live in glass houses should grow Phragmipedium orchids.

Beauty is in the eye of the beholder, and you have exceptionally beautiful eyes when you are looking at me.

ERRATUM: The phrase "or a nelk" in the previous fortune should have read "or an elk."

You have a hidden talent for macramé.

If a man offers you lint, check its quality before buying.

Your lucky animal is the Japanese beetle. Sorry about that.

Be strong like the oak and silent like the—well, like the oak.

DOG SEEKS MASTER with liberal views on suppertime issue. Tired of waiting. Have been waiting for suppertime now since little hand was on the two and big hand was on the seven. It's time for me to make a clean break and seek a master who's truly compatible. If you agree that suppertime has been postponed far too long, let's get to-gether. Contact "Cody" in care of this publication.

"ONE MAN'S TRASH is another man's treasure," says a wise and deservedly popular proverb. Mr. Mervyn Dankwater is therefore of-fering his garbage for sale at the very economical price of only $50 per pound. All garbage is neatly packaged in one-pound bags of varying size (trash is sold by weight, not by volume). Contact Mervyn Dankwater in care of this publication before Friday morning. After Friday morning, contact City of Pittsburgh Department of Environ-mental Services.

WANTED: CONSUMPTIVE SOPRANO to play in new Verdi pro-duction. Modern audiences demand realism in their operas, and our attempts to stage *Traviata* with healthy Violettas have met with indif-ferent success at best. Please do not apply if you are not already knock-ing on death's door. Reasonable medical bills paid. McKees Rocks Opera & Singing Telegram Co., McKees Rocks.

DR. BOLI'S ELEMENTARY READER.

The Teacher of Useful Accomplishments.

This man is Mr. Clark—
Mark Clark—
A gay young spark
Who likes to bark.
Hark!
Hark unto the bark
Of Mark.

Just for a lark,
When it gets dark,
Ask Mark
(Or, rather, Mr. Clark)
To teach you how to bark
Like Mark.

SCIENCE EXPERIMENTS
YOU CAN DO AT HOME.

Experiment 1.

Hold a banana in your hand about four feet above the floor. Let go of the banana. What happens to the banana? Does it hit the floor?

Now hold another banana in your hand about an inch above a wooden table. Let go of the banana. What happens to the banana? Does it hit the floor?

What this experiment proves: Wood has antigravitational properties.

Experiment 2.

Pour some water into a glass. What happens to the water? Does it stay in the glass?

Now turn the glass upside-down. What happens to the water? Does it stay in the glass?

What this experiment proves: Glass is a capricious substance and is not to be trusted.

Experiment 3.

Dial 9-1-1, ask for the paramedics, and tell them you think you are having a heart attack. Time how long it takes them to arrive.

Now dial 9-1-1, ask for the paramedics, and tell them you have a mild cold. Time how long it takes them to arrive.

What this experiment proves: Your local paramedics are lazy, inefficient, and judgmental.

Experiment 4.

Soak an old shirt in kerosene. Is the shirt on fire?

Now touch a lighted match to the kerosene-soaked shirt. Is the shirt on fire?

What this experiment proves: You should always have a fire extinguisher handy when you are performing science experiments at home. Also, you probably should not have annoyed the paramedics in Experiment 3.

"Then it is moved and seconded that the middle classes can go to blazes. All in favor..." (Page 1467.)

DR. BOLI'S AGE-DEFYING ELIXIR.

AT THE PRESENT time, Dr. Boli is just a month shy of 229 years old, but he is frequently mistaken for a man half his age. To what does he attribute his youthful vigor? The secret lies in Dr. Boli's Age-Defying Elixir, the receipt for which is now revealed to the public for the first time.

In a stout mixing bowl, combine

> 2 cups plain yogurt
> 1 tsp rose water
> 1 tsp turbinado sugar
> 1 tsp Hungarian paprika

Meanwhile, chop and discard

> 3 heads lettuce
> 3 heads endive
> 3 heads celery
> 3 heads old-fashioned oatmeal

In a small frying pan, roast

> 1 clay pigeon

until lightly salted.

To the yogurt mixture, add

2 cups confetti (mixed colors)

Stir gently while admiring the clay pigeon; then toss the mixture over the head of a passing prothonotary. When he pursues you, run like the wind. To this program of vigorous exercise Dr. Boli attributes all his much-remarked youth and vitality.

A GLOSSARY OF COMMON TERMS IN JOURNALISM.

Balanced. Giving equal weight to truth and falsehood.

Fair. Not actionably libelous.

Feature. A free advertisement for a business or organization run by the publisher's friend or relative.

Investigative reporting. A news story designed to embarrass one of the publisher's enemies.

Lead. An irrelevant paragraph inserted at the beginning of a news story to discourage readers from continuing. A classic example of a lead: "Cindy Lang never wanted to be leader of the Pittsburgh chapter of Parents of Murdered Children."

Lede. An alternate spelling of "lead," often used by journalists who don't rede much.

News analysis. A method of filling column inches when all the facts are obscure or unknown.

Objective. 1. Conforming to the writer's preconceived notion of the facts of the story. —2. Conforming to the copy editor's preconceived notion of the facts of the story. —3. Conforming to the publisher's pre-conceived notion of the facts of the story.

Quote. A short sentence that some public figure might have said if the journalist had been able to hear what he was saying.

Reliable source. A source whose statements are indefinite enough that they cannot be proved false.

Skewed. Demonstrably true, as opposed to *balanced.*

TONIGHT ON DUMONT.

Miss Rutherford Mysteries. When two slices of bacon go missing from Miss Rutherford's breakfast, Miss Rutherford suspects her dog Jem-mie. Starring Dame Wilhelmina Frimp as Miss Rutherford, with spe-cial guest Anthony Quagga as Jemmie. Check local listings.

THINGS TO DO WHILE SNOWBOUND
WITH NO HEAT OR ELECTRIC POWER.

WRITE A BIOGRAPHY of William Henry Harrison entirely from memory. Then use the old encyclopedia in the basement to see how close you came. Give yourself two points for every date you got right.

If you have a gas stove that you can light with a match, make a dinner using everything in the pantry that will fit in one pot. Call it a "gumbo." If challenged, explain that mangoes are traditional in the gumbo recipes of St. Pierre and Miquelon.

Make your own Internet out of tin cans and string.

Call the electric company and report an outage, but give a fictitious ad-dress. This provides the beleaguered telephone representatives with precious amusement to relieve the stress of the emergency.

Paint pictures on the television screen, then erase them and repaint them. If you do this thirty times a second, you will create the illusion that you are watching television.

Shiver. Award prizes for the best or most creative shivering.

Shake your fist at heaven. Use any resulting fire or brimstone to heat your house.

From LETTERS OF A POET OF PARIS.

Translated from *Lettres d'un poète parisien*,

by Udolphe de l'Ennui.

My dear L——,

SPRING HAS COME, and I feel the gentle breeze wafting through the open window. Petals flutter like pink fairy wings from the apple tree in the garden. How I hate the spring! It is worse than an abomination: it is a commonplace...

Did you imagine that I should be enchanted by your descriptions of the wines of Sauternes, which you call sweet as honey, with all the fruits of the orchard in the scent? Did you imagine that I cared for such things as honey or fruits? All sweetness is a monstrous lie; all fruit is stunningly audacious in its mendacity. Only in bitterness is there truth, because bitterness is the scent of death, and only in death is the truth of life revealed. I sup on wormwood: away with honey, and fruits, and marmalade, especially marmalade. Do not fail to send more of Mlle de V——'s excellent marmalade, so that I may despise it...

The greengrocer is pushing his cart up the street, singing happily to himself. The imbecile! What is it to me if he dances on the bridge at Avignon? I despise dancing, and I despise bridges. Nor do I care much for Avignon... The birds also are singing, and they are imbeciles as well, but they have the good sense not to dance, even on bridges...

The treacherous sun, with cowardly stealth, has inched its way across the sky again, and now floods my chamber with its rays. How it mocks me! It grows stronger little by little every day, while I must grow weaker for my art: weaker and weaker, wasting away. Already I have scarcely the life in me to get up and shut the blind... I lie on my couch, immobile, and I feel I must die; I know it. But send the marmalade anyway, in case I am wrong.

Yours in misery of soul,
Udolphe.

P.S.—Give my love to Mme L—— and all the little L——s.

My dear L——,

THE SUMMER BREEZES puff gently through my window this evening, carrying the sweet scents of a thousand blossoms from the tiny walled garden below. How I hate gardens, walled or otherwise! They are small outcroppings of paradise, and a poet has nothing to do with paradise; a poet must be damned to hell for eternity, or he is a mere bourgeois doggerel-monger. How I wish the world would despise my poetry, so that I should know myself to be a true poet! Yet the latest review in the *Artichaut quotidien* calls my poetry "damnable." You see how impossible it is for a poet to rise up against the establishment, when the establishment appreciates him for what he is....

The bourgeois scents of the bourgeois flowers Mme La Salle has planted cause me to think of death. A thousand times a day I think of death: death, whose embrace is sweeter than the madeleines in the Rue du Nom Disyllable; death, whose icy breath I feel even now on my knee (for you must know that I have infernally cold knees, even at the height of summer); yet death will not come, and I am compelled to live. To live! What a hollow endeavor it is to live, when every attempt at it must at the last end in failure! Only a bourgeois mind could find satisfaction in mere living. Yet sometimes I wonder whether, when it finally comes for me, death will not prove to be bourgeois as well....

The world grows darker, and for a moment I think my bosom-companion death has remembered me at last; but no, it is merely that the sun has set, which by some cruel law of nature which no one understands deprives me of the light from my window. There are philosophers who make the bold claim that they understand this thing, but they understand nothing. Only in poetry is there truth: in poetry and in death, wherefore to know the truth it is necessary to be either a poet or dead, and preferably both....

I must end this letter now. The light is failing; and, if I light a lamp, Mme La Salle will know that I am at home and will pester me with her endless bourgeois questions about the rent. Does she suppose that such a mundane subject as rent would be of interest to me? Farewell! I must now sit in the darkness and think of death, and of madeleines. Perhaps there is hope; perhaps it is possible to die of a surfeit of madeleines. I must attempt the experiment....

Yours in misery of soul,

Udolphe

P.S.—I hope Mme L—— and all the little L——s are well.

My dear L——,

AUTUMN IS COME, with its crisp air and brightly colored leaves. Of such tawdry clichés is nature capable! I despise nature, as I despise everything in Art that is not natural. It is the duty of Art to be true to nature, and only what is natural in Art is praiseworthy. But what is natural in nature is merely commonplace...

Mme La Salle is demanding the rent again, though it is hardly a month since she last demanded it, the greedy bourgeois hussy... I despise her filthy bourgeois greed, and I despise this filthy bourgeois apartment. Yesterday I flung soup at the ceiling to make it filthier, so that I might despise it the more. I tell myself that one must live somewhere, yet something within me asks why—why must one live somewhere instead of nowhere?... This morning Mme La Salle came in and cleaned the soup stains while I was out. She has ruined a good day's despising...

I was out this morning because I was eating madeleines at the café on the Rue du Nom Disyllable. I despise the empty allurements of bourgeois pastries. But I think I do not despise madeleines as much as I despise the rest. This has provoked a crisis of conscience...

Soon the winter will be upon us, that annual reminder of our mortality, grim metaphor for death. I despise metaphor; and therefore I despise the winter, because it is metaphorical. A season that has not the courage to say what it means directly is despicable;—nay, more than despicable: it is bourgeois. I despise bourgeois seasons as I despise bourgeois bourgeois, with their filthy greed and their petty talk of nothing but money. I know, my dear old friend, that you despise money as much as I do, which you might easily demonstrate by sending 120 francs for the rent.

Yours in misery of soul,

Udolphe.

P.S.—As always, give my love to Mme L—— and all the little L——s.

ANNOUNCEMENT.

ENHANCED SECURITY MEASURES now being implemented at our nation's airports may make it necessary for authorized Transportation Security Administration staff to dress certain randomly selected passengers in the chicken suit. Please remember that these measures are for your own safety, as well as the safety of your fellow passengers. Your full cooperation is appreciated.

THE LITTLE DUTCH BOY WHO SAVED HOLLAND.

From *Dr. Boli's Fables for Children*
Who Are Too Old to Believe in Fables.

ONCE THERE WAS a little Dutch boy who discovered a leak in the dike.

What should he do? From a single leak, a terrible breach might grow. The whole country could be flooded, and everyone he knew would drown.

So he did the only thing he could think of. He stuck his finger in the dike, and the leak stopped.

Of course, now he was stuck. He couldn't move, because as soon as he did, the leak would start again.

So he stood there for quite some time. He was rather tired, and his finger felt a bit numb from the effort of holding back the North Sea, but he knew he was doing his duty.

At last the Burgomaster happened to pass by.

"Young man," he said with a certain amount of sternness, "why are you poking your finger in the dike?"

"I am stopping a leak," the boy explained. "I saw the dike leaking, so I stuck my finger in the hole."

"Heroic boy!" the Burgomaster exclaimed. "You shall be rewarded! Meanwhile, keep your finger there while I call the Burghers together."

So the Burgomaster called a meeting of the Burghers, and they agreed that the boy had heroically saved Holland.

"And now," the Burgomaster asked, "what shall we do about the leak?"

"It seems to me," one of the Burghers replied, "that private enterprise has already found an admirable solution to the problem. The boy has stuck his finger in the dike, and the leak has stopped. You might describe it as voluntary self-regulation. There is no need for expensive government action."

So the Burghers voted to award the boy a Certificate of Good Citizenship, which the Burgomaster was delighted to be able to present to him the next day.

"Thank you," the boy said politely, "but I still have my finger in this dike."

"And we appreciate that," the Burgomaster replied. "I may confidently speak for the whole Council of Burghers in saying that your heroic action is universally admired."

So the boy stood there with his finger in the dike for a few more days.

It was not long, however, before another leak sprang in the dike, a little bit farther down the way.

"What shall we do?" the Burgomaster asked the Burghers. "There is another leak."

"As private enterprise has so admirably solved the previous problem," one of the Burghers responded, "the solution to this new leak is obvious. We need only persuade another heroic boy to stick his finger in it."

So they went into the local school and found another boy who, after much persuasion, was willing to stick his finger in the dike.

It was, however, only a few days later that two more leaks appeared. This time it was much harder to persuade boys to stick their fingers in the holes; and when, a week later, half a dozen more leaks appeared, no volunteers were to be found.

"What shall we do?" the Burgomaster asked the Council. "Private enterprise seems no longer to be adequate. We may have to repair the dike itself this time."

"Nonsense," said one of the Burghers. "The solution that worked before will work again. We must simply force private enterprise into action."

So the Council visited the school and dragged a number of young boys by the ears to the dike, where they were forced to plug the leaks with their fingers.

But the dike, which was old and poorly maintained, continued to spring new leaks here and there, so that it was all the Burghers could do to find more boys to plug up the leaks with their fingers. At last the Burghers compelled every little boy in the Low Countries to stick his finger in a hole. All economic activity came to a halt, as it is well known that young boys are the leading consumers of skates and cheese, on which the economy of Holland depended at that time.

"What shall we do?" the Burgomaster asked the Council. "We have run out of heroic little boys. At this rate, we may have to plug the leaks with our own fingers."

"That would be moderately inconvenient," one of the Burghers remarked.

So the Council voted to remove the North Sea by digging a new seabed somewhere in Germany; and they voted themselves a number of solid gold spades, befitting their dignity, for the purpose. And if you go to suburban Wilhelmshaven right now, and look into the field to your right as you drive westward on the Friedenstrasse, you will see a number of Dutch burghers very busy with their spades, trying to dig a new bed for the North Sea. It is lucky for them that the people of Wilhelmshaven have mistaken the burghers for a party of archaeologists looking for ancient Saxon remains, which has allowed them to continue the work uninterrupted.

NEW BACTERI*MATE is the humane alternative to antibiotics. Harmlessly traps bacteria for safe release in the wild. Little Friends Pest Control, Point Breeze.

THE BLUE KNIGHT.

Oh, you can search hither, and you can search thither,
And you can search over and under and through,
But no one knows whether, and no one knows whither
The Blue Knight has gone with his Mystic Kazoo.
    Oh, whether or whither,
    Or hither or thither—
Oh, where has he gone with his Mystic Kazoo?

In olden days (golden days), roughly and readily
Knights in bright armor all knew what to do;
And no knight did better than, slowly and steadily,
That magical Knight with his Mystic Kazoo.
    Oh, roughly and readily,
    Slowly and steadily,
Where has he gone with his Mystic Kazoo?

Five nights in a row, as I paced on the ceiling,
Five knights in a row hummed along while he blew
A rare old Allegro with infinite feeling,
As only he could, on his Mystic Kazoo.
    I still pace the ceiling,
    But not with such feeling—
Oh, where has he gone with his Mystic Kazoo?

For five afternoons, while I danced on the shrubbery,
He blew forth his melodies, sacred and true;
Five knights backed him up with cow-bells and wash-tubbery,
But no other knight knew the Mystic Kazoo.
    I've flattened the shrubbery,
    Lost the wash-tubbery—
Where has he gone with his Mystic Kazoo?

Five mornings, lost mornings, at dawn's early rising,
I woke to the sound of a dairy-cow's moo;
The cow seemed annoyed, which was hardly surprising:
Beside her the Knight blew his Mystic Kazoo.
    Now there's nothing surprising
    At dawn's early rising.
Oh, where has he gone with his Mystic Kazoo?

I hung from the floorboards all evening one morning,
Enchanted as melodies fluttered and flew;
Alas, had I known he was blowing a warning,
I'd have begged him to stay with his Mystic Kazoo!
    I hung there all morning
    And missed his plain warning—
Oh, where has he gone with his Mystic Kazoo?

And now knights are fewer, and nights are all longer,
And days have grown grayer, as days often do,
And summer grows weaker, and winter grows stronger,
And all for the lack of a Mystic Kazoo!

Spring weaker, fall stronger,
Days shorter, nights longer—
Oh, where has he gone with his Mystic Kazoo?

And we've looked up and down till we're starting to blither;
We've checked Manitoba, Dubai, and Peru,
But no one knows whether, and no one knows whither
The Blue Knight has gone with his Mystic Kazoo.
Oh, look till you blither,
But no one knows whither—
Oh, where has he gone with his Mystic Kazoo?

"Don't be so morbidly suspicious, darling. You know a wise wife prepares for any eventuality." (Page 482.)

UNEXPLAINED PHENOMENA.

ONE OF THE atomic clocks at Carnegie-Mellon University consistently resets itself to Newfoundland time at midnight every April 10.

On September 12, 1927, at about 1:15 in the afternoon, a silver Walking Liberty half-dollar left by Mr. Ernest Plinck on the counter of the Standard Diner in Wilkes-Barre, Penna., vanished without a trace.

An elevator in the Benedum-Trees Building goes only up.

It has been well established by ornithologists that barn swallows do not build their own barns, but no one knows how the barns have come to be.

Every morning since November 3, 1946, guards opening up the City-County Building for the day's business have found a single sterling-silver seafood fork on the mat just inside the left-hand door.

It was said that the late Rev. Herbert Clang of St. Ronald's could levitate, but only in the small hours of the morning, and that he used his miraculous powers to change burnt-out light bulbs in the sanctuary.

No one knows why Madder Purple is so much angrier than the other colors in the paintbox.

A parrot raised from birth by Ms. Edwina Trundle of Troy Hill speaks only Malayalam, though Ms. Trundle herself is unacquainted with the language.

At some time on the morning of April 4, 1978, three custard-filled doughnuts left in the office refrigerator by Mr. Wendell H. Wendell disappeared without a trace. They have never been seen again.

The "Redbud" tree, *Cercis canadensis*, has buds that are deep magenta, not red.

A 1975 Dodge Dart in the possession of Miss Rosamund Clifford-Jones of Paris, Va., has the left taillight of a 1975 Plymouth Valiant.

In some provincial colleges and universities, "deconstructionism" is still taken seriously.

Southbound drivers on West Virginia highway 218 invariably burst out laughing at a point 2.4 miles north of Worthington, but are never able afterwards to account for their hilarity.

A German shepherd belonging to Ms. Thaddea Ingraham of Davenport, Iowa, responds only to commands in the Fortran computer programming language.

In spite of decades of experimentation and research, electrical engineers have never succeeded in explaining how fluorescent lights work.

The famous Old Trothless geyser outside Battered Spoon, Wyoming, has never erupted once in recorded history.

Mr. Regis T. Quandary, a regular Friday-night patron at Krzrnpski's Tavern on the South Side, has observed numerous incidents of bilocation among other patrons at the bar, but scientists so far have refused to take his testimony seriously.

In the middle 1970s, thousands of apparently healthy people began to care for small stones as if they were domestic pets, even training them to obey commands like "stay" and "sit." To this day no cause has been assigned to what some have described as the largest mass delusion in modern history.

During the appearance of Halley's Comet in 1835, all the sweet corn in Lebanon County, Penna., suddenly turned yellow. Until that time all varieties of sweet corn had been white; the famous "Yellow Comet Corn" is the ancestor of all our yellow varieties.

In Shamokin, Penna., the sun rises in the west and sets in the east every third Tuesday in May.

Atlantic perch are born left-handed, but since they have no hands this anomaly escaped the attention of ichthyologists until recently.

A flurry of absolutely identical snowflakes fell over Bangor, Me., in February of 1877.

The LaFond twins, Napoleon and Louis Philippe, became famous in the 1930s for their ability to communicate telepathically, but only when a radio station nearby was transmitting programming from the NBC Blue Network.

Nostradamus predicted the career of Duke Ellington with otherwise perfect accuracy, but somehow failed to mention Barney Bigard.

The Mourning Dove (*Zenaida macroura*) was once noted for its infallible ability to find any Esso station within fifty miles of its migration route, but since the disappearance of that brand has been unable to migrate at all.

Researchers applying modern forensic sound-restoration techniques to the notorious 18-minute gap in Richard Nixon's presidential tapes have uncovered a sound that one expert identifies as someone tuning a mandolin.

"Mavis," a mixed-breed dog belonging to Mr. Reginald van Bagg of Upper Sandusky, has been digging in the same spot in the back yard since September of 2007 without ever finding what she was looking for.

A stone excavated during the extension of the Sviatoshynsko-Brovarska line in the Kiev metro in 1978 was such a stunningly exact likeness of Leonid Brezhnev that it was immediately vandalized beyond recognition.

The so-called "Middle Ages" came very near the end of the 200,000 years or so of human history.

A statue of the Blessed Virgin in St. Britney Church has been observed to begin weeping every week at the precise moment when the
guitars are brought out of their cases for the contemporary Mass.

BLANKETS, THROWS, AFGHANS, shawls, slipcovers, rebosos,
etc., hand-woven from the finest Armenian string cheese. Sent in re-
frigerated carton for optimum freshness. The Dari-Weave Corp.,
Larimer.

COOKING FOR ONE.

HERE WE ARE again with Herb's Cooking for One, the show where
we cook things guys like to eat. I'm Al, filling in for Herb, who's starting to get some of his hair back, at least in spots, so things are really
coming along there.

Today we're going to make something a lot of guys like to have for
lunch. It's called *peanut butter and jelly*, and I'll bet your mom used to
make it for you. But some guys don't live with their moms anymore, so
I'm going to show you how you can make it for yourself. It gets a bit
tricky in places, so pay attention. I don't want any letters from per-
sonal-injury attorneys like I got when I showed you how to make
chocolate milk, okay? So here we go.

Now, the first thing you need is some bread. Normal bread comes in
slices like these right here, but if you're not careful you can end up
with bread where they've stuck all the slices together with glue or
something, so it's like just one big lump of bread. I was over at my
fancy-pants sister's house the other day, and she had bread like that,
and she had to use a knife to get the slices apart. I said, Why don't
they just leave the slices apart in the first place, instead of sticking
them together like that? She looked at me like I was crazy. Women,
huh? They always make everything ten times more complicated than
it has to be.

So we have our peanut butter over here, and our jelly over here, and
there's a reason for that, so pay attention. Now, you see how I'm
putting these two slices of bread side by side like this? That's cause

the peanut butter goes on the right side, and the jelly goes on the left side. That's what my mother taught me, and that's what I believe. You don't want to get your peanut butter on the left like some sort of commie pinko Islamofascist liberal atheist nazi Mormon. So you take your knife—I mean the dull kind you find in the silverware drawer, not the sharp kind, cause if your wife is like mine she won't even tell you where the sharp ones are anymore—and you stick it in the jar and come out with some peanut butter. And then you sort of smear it all over the bread, like this. It's sort of like laying bricks, except you don't want to lay bricks with peanut butter, cause I can tell you from experience that doesn't work.

Then we do the jelly. Some people say they can get the jelly out of the jar with a knife, too, but I never can. It always slides off. I mean, maybe if you're a brain surgeon you can do that, but what I always do is turn the jar over above the bread and bang it like this until some comes out. I just keep banging it like this, and some more, and—well, there, that was most of the jar, but that's all right cause I like jelly.

So now you've got your peanut butter on the right and your jelly on the left, and I know what you're thinking. You're thinking, "Which side does the mayonnaise go on?" Well, obviously it goes on the right. I mean, that's way easier than trying to make it stick to a great big pile of jelly.

Well, that's all we have time for right now, so you're just going to have to figure out how to put the halves together yourselves. Keep those cards and letters coming for Herb, and I want you to know his nurse reads every single one of them, although she doesn't understand them very well unless they're in Ukrainian. Until next time, this is Al, saying what Herb always says, which is, "Remember, cooking is for guys, too."

THE ADVENTURES OF SIR MONTAGUE BLASTOFF, INTERPLANETARY SPACE DRAGOON.

ANNOUNCER. And now Malt-O-Cod, the only malt food drink flavored with real cod-liver oil, proudly presents...

(*Music: Fanfare*)

ANNOUNCER. The Adventures of Sir Montague Blastoff, Interplanetary Space Dragoon!

(*Music: Theme, in and under for...*)

ANNOUNCER. Tonight we find Sir Montague busy as always, with Colonel Wilhelmina Darling by his side.

SIR MONTAGUE. I say, could you give us a hand with this?

COL. DARLING. What do you need, Monty?

SIR MONTAGUE. It's these quarterly reports. I've been racking my brain trying to remember whether our battle with the Wombat People was before or after five in the evening. I wasn't exactly watching the clock, you know.

COL. DARLING. Does it really matter?

SIR MONTAGUE. Well, of course it matters, my dear. If it was after five, then it goes on form 398-B, not A, and everyone must be paid time and a half overtime.

COL. DARLING. In that case, it was definitely after five.

SIR MONTAGUE. Are you quite sure? Wouldn't want to get a thing like that wrong, you know.

COL. DARLING. I may be only nineteen and ravishingly beautiful, but I am also a colonel in the 58th Interplanetary Space Dragoons. My word is my bond.

SIR MONTAGUE. Very well, then. Now, when I rescued you from the wicked Viscount Van Allen Flogg, did you remember to file Form 8340-M, Escape from Fate Worse than Death?

COL. DARLING. Oh, Monty, can you doubt me after all our precious moments together?

SIR MONTAGUE. I'll take that as a yes, then, which is jolly fortunate. Saves a rotten lot of paperwork if you did. Now, after we were lost for three weeks on the Dragon Sands of the planet Bingo and we had to eat our own boots, did you remember to fill out all the proper Disposition of Footwear forms when we got back?

COL. DARLING. You know I did, Monty. I'd do anything for you.

SIR MONTAGUE. And a fine thing, too. I like having someone I can jolly well rely on to take care of the old paperwork. "That Colonel Darling," I always say to myself—"what a fine bureaucratic mind she has."

COL. DARLING. But, Monty, don't you ever think of me in any other way?

SIR MONTAGUE. Well, of course, you do make a dashed fine gin and tonic. Never could quite get the recipe right myself.

COL. DARLING. But, Monty, don't you have—you know—feelings for me?

SIR MONTAGUE. Feelings?

COL. DARLING. I may be a colonel in the 58th Interplanetary Space Dragoons, but I am also nineteen and ravishingly beautiful. Surely you must have noticed that my heaving bosom swells with billows of love.

SIR MONTAGUE. I say! Do you mean to tell me you're in love with me?

COL. DARLING. Always and forever, Monty! I've been in love with you since the moment you whisked me away from the death pits of the Ant-Lion People!

SIR MONTAGUE. Well, dash it all.

COL. DARLING (*shocked and hurt*). Why, Monty, how could you react that way?

SIR MONTAGUE. Well, it means another bally load of forms to fill out, that's all. I say, could you give us a hand with them?

(*Music: Theme, in and under for...*)

ANNOUNCER. Don't miss next week's exciting episode: *Sir Montague Blastoff vs. the Department of Motor Vehicles!* Till then, remember to pester your parents for Malt-O-Cod every day. It's the only malt food drink with the rich, satisfying flavor of real cod-liver oil, now with the exclusive Sir Montague Blastoff pocket financial calculator in every package. It's the malt food drink that's brain food—Malt-O-Cod!

(*Music: In full, then out.*)

DR. BOLI'S ENCYCLOPEDIA OF MISINFORMATION,
Great Cities of the United States Edition.

Boston. Beginning this season, the swan boats on the Lagoon in the Public Gardens will no longer be made from real swans.

Chicago. In Chicago, a "Chicago-style" hot dog is known as a "Fort Wayne frank."

Los Angeles. Many Southern Californians mistakenly believe that Los Angeles is counted among the great cities of the United States.

New York. Since the borough of Manhattan was sold to Disney last year, much progress has been made in clearing out the undesirable poor; and it is estimated that no one with an annual income of less than $400,000 will be left on the island by 2015.

Philadelphia. The old rule that no structure in the city of Philadelphia may be taller than William Penn's hat is still in force, but it has been necessary to place the hat itself on an 84-storey pole to accommodate current tastes in architecture.

Pittsburgh. The new subway station beside PNC Park has been deliberately built deeper under the ground than any other station in Pittsburgh so that Pirates fans may sneak away unobserved after a game.

Washington. No one was bold enough to tell the venerable and beloved President Washington that he had made an elementary blunder in surveying; and as a result of the unfortunate reticence of his staff, our capital city ended up being built in a swamp along the Potomac.

NEW EDUCATIONAL FILM. "Our Friend the Elbow" teaches proper elbow care & hygiene in an entertaining yet sensitive manner. Sure to be in demand for high-school health classes, where frankness tempered with a certain degree of delicacy is necessary in approaching this controversial topic. Available in Super 8 as well as standard 16mm. Perrysville Puppet Theater Educational Films, Perrysville.

A LETTER

From the Tri-Borough Home Loan Association.

"Brutus"
152 Brake Street
Wilmerding, Penna.

Dear Mr. Brutus:

It has come to our attention that you are a dog. Under those circum-stances, we believe it is in the best interest both of our Association and of you yourself that we should withdraw the offer we made to you in our previous correspondence. The "Make-a-Wish" Home Improve-ment Loan program is designed primarily for human beings who are homeowners and have built up some equity in their properties. It is not generally suitable for the somewhat different lifestyle of dogs or other domestic animals, who do not accumulate real property in the same way under the laws of this Commonwealth.

Instead, may we interest you in the "Bones & Rags" Equity Loan program? This program is specifically designed to transform the half-chewed toys, old shoes, tennis balls, and sticks you may have accumu-lated into assets you can draw on to pay for a new doghouse roof, a better collar, or even just a bag of pig ears to chew on. Right now rates on canine equity loans are at an all-time low, so there's never been a better time to take advantage of this unique opportunity. If you're interested, stop by our office in Turtle Creek any weekday between 10 a.m. and 4 p.m. and ask for Fluffy.

Yours sincerely,
Thaddeus Ramshackle III,
Vice President,
Tri-Borough Home Loan Association.

IN ART NEWS.

ARTIST RUPERT SLACKSTRIPE, who painted Cirencester beige, has been arrested on charges of simple assault after he attempted to apply spray-paint to five visitors to the Duck Hollow Museum of Art. Through a spokesman, Slackstripe described the charges as "a triumph of philistinism." The spokesman said that the spray-painting was part of a work of art entitled *To the Nth Degree*, which requires unwilling participants to make its point. The misdemeanor assault charges represent a significant stylistic departure for Slackstripe, most of whose previous works have been felonies.

DIRE PREDICTIONS.

SCIENTISTS NOW BELIEVE, based on the latest astronomical observations, that the end of the world will come at precisely the most
inconvenient time.

China will soon surpass the United States in number of inert citizens
watching game shows on television.

The number of radio receivers is rapidly increasing in the developing
world, and scientists estimate that they will have sucked up all the radio waves by 2019.

If the human population continues to expand, future settlers may be
forced to repopulate Detroit or Youngstown.

At the current rate of depletion, the Internet will run out of cat pictures by 2027.

When we run out of coal, Santa Claus may be forced to bring uranium
ore to naughty children.

If transit ridership continues to increase, the federal government will
be forced to support the automobile industry by buying luxury SUVs
for intransigent transit riders, at enormous cost to the taxpayer.

By the time you finish reading this article, the future you dread will have already begun.

IN ENTERTAINMENT NEWS.

THE FOLGER SHAKESPEARE Library has announced a new project called "Shakespeare Rebooted," which will bring Shakespeare up to contemporary standards of storytelling. The project aims to provide a new timeline for the Shakespearean universe that will place all of Shakespeare's characters in a consistent world. The first production is a Hamlet prequel entitled *Aye, Claudius!*, which will reveal the tragic origin story of the "Claudius" supervillain character.

DR. BOLI'S LIBRARY OF LOST BOOKS.

Atlas of the Noses of Africa, in Comparison with the Pure Nordic Type, by Sir Trismegistus Ashen.

AS ONE OF the chief authorities in nineteenth-century ethnography, Sir Trismegistus Ashen was a figure whose works were much anticipated when they were announced, and often cited once they had appeared in print. There was accordingly much excited murmuring in the intellectual world when Sir Trismegistus declared his intention of traveling to Africa to gather material for a new study to be called An Atlas of the Noses of Africa, in Comparison with the Pure Nordic Type.

Sir Trismegistus was widely regarded, not least by himself, as the foremost authority on noses in the field of ethnography. It was his contention that the distinctive nose of the Northern European proved his superiority to the men of all other races.

"The Nordic or Teutonic nose," he wrote in the *Proceedings of the All-British Philethnographic Society*, "taken in its pure form as a distinct type, is conspicuously longer, and correspondingly more sensitive, than the olfactory organs of other racial types. The superior length of the nose renders it a delicate instrument for the detection of subtle odors at a distance, for which reason the degree of development of that organ may be taken as indicative of a given race's position on the evolutionary scale." A short nose on an Englishman or Prussian he regarded as indicative of an impure or adulterate ancestry, and there-fore a mark of inferiority. It goes without saying that the nose of Sir Trismegistus was positively enormous.

Upon his arrival in George Town, then the administrative capital of the British Protectorate of Northern Southwest East Africa, Sir Tris-megistus was provided by the colonial authorities with a large contin-gent of native bearers, all of whose noses were duly measured, for the carriage of his equipment and supplies. With this train he set out at once into the interior, measuring noses at every stop. A few of the na-tives objected to having their noses prodded with rulers and squeezed with calipers, and Sir Trismegistus' letters from the expedition narrate more than one hair's-breadth escape from an angry native who misun-derstood his benign intentions. More often, however, his subjects re-ceived him hospitably and patiently endured his measurements.

Contrary to what he had expected when he began his expedition, Sir Trismegistus discovered that Africa was blessed with a wealth of nasal types. "I have discovered," he wrote in one of his letters, "in ad-dition to the short noses which I had expected to find, whole tribes with noses of the purest Teutonic type, as well as any number of inter-mediate noses. This variation can only have been produced by an ad-mixture of the African and Teutonic races in prehistoric times. I be-lieve I am the first to have discovered this evidence of these hitherto unsuspected voyages of our remote ancestors, the knowledge of which must add greatly to our appreciation of the superiority of the Nordic race."

At last, having measured thousands of noses in his more than two years of wandering throughout the interior of Africa, Sir Trismegistus came to a village of the M'numu people, where he was introduced to a local sage or shaman who very politely asked permission to measure his thumb.

"I am compiling a monograph," the M'numu scholar explained as he took careful measurements of length and circumference, "to be entitled *A Compendium of the Thumbs of the European Explorers, with Reference to the Pure African Type*. Most Europeans have stubby little thumbs, indicative of their racial inferiority when compared with the long and agile thumb of the African. The thumb, you see, is the organ by which tools are manipulated, for which reason we may regard the comparative development of the thumb as indicative of a given race's position on the evolutionary scale. Your thumb, I might mention, is quite long, and very nearly of the pure African type, pointing to some admixture of African blood in your ancestry, of which you must be justifiably proud."

In the evening, Sir Trismegistus announced his intention to terminate the expedition. The next morning, as he was boarding the boat that would take him down to the mouth of the M'numu River, he tripped over one of the many shaggy dogs that wandered free in the village; and, as he pitched forward, the bound folio volume containing all his two years of nasal observations fell into the river. His companions reported later that he made no serious effort to retrieve it.

IN THE NEWS.

UNDER THE IMPRESSION that he was joining the John Birch Society, Mr. Oswald Theodoric "Theo" Wren, the noted anti-immigra-
tion activist, discovered last night that he had mistakenly joined a similarly named club devoted to recreational flogging, whose members,
oddly enough, were mostly immigrants from Guatemala and El Sal-
vador. Mr. Wren is listed in serious but stable condition at Memorial
Hospital and is expected to make a full recovery, with the exception of
a slight impairment in his dignity.

A "WHITE PRIDE" rally downtown erupted in chaos this morning
when it was discovered that the caterer had inadvertently supplied the
sandwiches on whole-wheat bread instead of white. None of the fourteen participants in the rally were injured, but witnesses reported seeing the sidewalk smeared with mayonnaise for as much as half a block.

"Well, I could try playing some ragtime instead." (Page 1193.)

KNOW YOUR FIBER.

EVERYONE KNOWS THAT fiber is essential to good health. But how much do you really know about fiber? Test your knowledge with these fiber questions:

1. *What is dietary fiber?*

Dietary fiber is the fiber we eat in our diets. Honestly, if you didn't get this one, you really are a bit thick.

2. *Where do we get fiber?*

Fiber comes from the socks, old rags, and handkerchiefs we eat every day.

3. *Can we get fiber from fruits and vegetables?*

We can if the fruits and vegetables are packed in burlap sacks, and we do not neglect to eat the burlap.

4. *What do we need fiber for?*

The fiber we eat forms itself into a clump that scours the insides of our intestines, getting rid of all the hair and soap scum that build up in there and ensuring free-flowing drainage.

5. Why do the British spell it "fibre"?

The Norman Conquest infected the British Isles with a certain quantity of Frenchified spellings for words like "fibre" and "colour." Since the Normans never conquered America, the United States preserves the original correct spellings of these words.

From THE VIRTUOUS CHILD'S STORY-BOOK.

"MAMMA, I GAVE a penny to a poor man this morning. Was I a good boy for so doing?'

"It depends on the motive you had in view. Did you give it to him because you thought it would do him good?"

"Yes, mamma, I did; for I saw that he was miserable and unhappy, and when I passed him he held out his hat and begged for a penny so that he could buy a trifle to eat. So I thought of the penny I had in my pocket, and I said to myself, 'Perhaps with my penny he can buy some food, and then he will not be so miserable.'"

"I am sorry to hear it, my dear boy. This is what you should have thought: 'This man is poor and in dire need, and I possess the means whereby to sustain his life for another day. This possession gives me the power to place him forever in my debt, and to bind him by invisible chains to do my will in hopes of gaining the penny, which after all I may not give to him if I am not pleased with him. And with the profit I make from his servitude I may purchase the lives of multitudes of similar beggars, and gradually form myself an army of shuffling automatons whose very existence depends on my pleasure.'"

"Ah! mamma, I wish I had thought of that, but I am sure I did not intend to do wrong. You know, mamma, I love you so dearly, that I strive to please you in all things."

"Yes, my dear, I know you love me, and that is because I hold your wretched little life in my hands, is it not? So think, dear child, when next you meet a beggar, what unimaginable power the single penny in your pocket gives you over the wretched lives of those less fortunate than yourself, and you will make me proud of you."

INTERVIEW.
(From the Late City Edition of the Dispatch.)

DR. EMIL WOLFSPITZ *has just been named the new director of Rogerian Therapists Without Borders, an organization that provides Rogerian psychotherapy to those in need in war zones and disaster areas worldwide. The Dispatch was granted an exclusive interview with Dr. Wolfspitz yesterday in his office in the Benedum-Trees Building.*

Dispatch. What do you anticipate will be your greatest challenge as you take up the leadership of the organization?

Dr. Wolfspitz. You want to know what I anticipate will be my greatest challenge as I take up the leadership of the organization.

N.B.—*At this point, the Dispatch determined that it would be in the best interest of our readers to terminate the interview.*

A POEM,

entitled "Ode to a Very Good Article," constructed from comments sub-
mitted but for various reasons not approved for publication. Each stanza
is originally one entire comment.

COUNTRY MEET BOSOM friend,
all within the four seas are brothers,
the author of the article let me remember profoundly,
writing is very good.

Unmatchable aspiring an dwelling house
misrepresenting consequence
because the crime syndicate.
An vacation or an exceptional social occasion
embodies a good fourth dimension.

Statements unobstructed,
at the beginning and the end of the handle
is very good,
is a very good article.

I experienced it's helpful to me,
I hope every volition like it.

Your information inch this article to partake in,

service me.
Incisively what I needed.
I remember the author's composition
constitutes really effective,
whilst the point of panorama
a minuscule morsel contrasting,
simply izzit is a good article,
and the source give the sack
trust to feature sentence
to talk about close to troubles.

The music is not pleasing to the ear;
we might have more of the grand rhythm
and majestic Louis Vuitton Monogram Purse the Ganges,
flowing slowly and eternally into the sea.

Be courageous in your life
and in your pursuit of the things you want
and the timberland shoes outlet person
you want to become.

Finally, I seemed to grasp his meaning
and realized that here was
a profound observation wholesale timberland boots.

ONE SIMPLE RULE FOR
GRADUATE STUDY IN LITERATURE.

A LOYAL READER who prefers to remain anonymous writes:

> Since he himself has successfully attained his doctor-
> ate, I've long wished that Dr. Boli would set forth
> his rules for graduate study in literature.

Dr. Boli is always happy to oblige a reader. Although Dr. Boli earned his own doctorates by unconventional and probably more honest means, he has observed that there is one rule that will assure the student of success and even acclaim in graduate study of literature:

Any text, studied long enough and in sufficient depth, becomes pseudonymous.

Did Dickens really write *A Tale of Two Cities?* Superficially, the work seems to bear many of the marks of his authorship. But is it not striking that nowhere else in Dickens' considerable oeuvre do we find a novel set during the French Revolution? Nor did Dickens ever begin any of his *undoubted* novels with a sentence that included the word best and the word worst in such near proximity; in fact, we can only describe the juxtaposition as entirely uncharacteristic, as a statistical analysis of Dickens' vocabulary will doubtless prove, after we have spent a full academic year putting it together. Henceforth the attribution of the work to Dickens must be regarded as a pious fiction, by which a much-beloved work of unknown authorship was attributed to the great man by his most loyal followers many years into the post-Dickensian age. As to the true authorship of the work, that is a matter, at present, of mere speculation; although it is suggestive that Thomas Love Peacock, in a remarkable echo of our unknown author, began one of his unpublished letters with the word "It." Until further work is done, we must refer to the author of *A Tale of Two Cities* as "Pseudo-Dickens."

You see how easy it is to apply this rule to any arbitrary work of literature. Go forth now and earn your well-deserved doctorate by the traditional means, if you must. As an alternative, however, you may wish to keep the Boli Institute in mind.

SUSPICIOUS ACTIVITIES.

IF YOU SEE anyone in your neighborhood engaging in any of these *suspicious activities*, call your local office of the Department of Home-land Security at once. If you do not know the number of your local Homeland Security office, stand at your bedroom window and wave your arm broadly back and forth three times, and an authorized Homeland Security agent will call you within fifteen seconds.

Driving over the speed limit. Terrorists often break speed laws in an attempt to escape from the scene of one of their failed atrocities.

Driving at or under the speed limit. Terrorists are often unusually ob-servant of speed laws in an attempt to avoid detection.

Owning a vehicle capable of transporting toxic chemicals, such as (for example) an automobile.

Using maps. Good citizens always know where they are going and how to get there.

Photographing historic buildings. Terrorists often use photographs of historic buildings to blackmail historic figures.

Debating controversial issues. Anyone who holds opinions different from yours on political or social issues is obviously up to something.

Refusing to sign up for the local supermarket's loyalty card. No innocent citizen with nothing to hide refuses to enjoy the many benefits of supermarket loyalty-card programs.

Reading long classic novels. No one actually reads *Moby Dick* or *War and Peace.* The books are probably explosive devices.

Not attracting attention. If someone is not doing anything unusual and appears in all respects perfectly normal, it is probably a terrorist trying not to look suspicious.

REMEMBER: Our department will be funded at its current level ONLY if everyone maintains a state of constant paranoid vigilance. KEEP ALERT AT ALL TIMES.

THE ASTONISHING WORLD OF TOMORROW.

WHAT MIGHT THE world be like one hundred years from today? The march of progress will bring such wonders as our generation can scarcely imagine, although our children's children will regard them as merely commonplace. With the help of leading researchers in every field, Dr. Boli brings you a glimpse of the astonishing world of 2111.

The Internet will be mostly printed on paper, eliminating the viruses and trojans that plague it today. Information will be arranged according to the order of the letters of the alphabet, so that no complex and unreliable "search engine" will be needed to find it.

Facilities for the preparation of food will be available in every home. Instead of purchasing standardized meals in frozen form or in paper bags from fast-food outlets, families will be able to produce for themselves nearly any kind of meal they desire, according to their own taste and requirements.

Motor vehicles capable of carrying hundreds of passengers at a time will move at speeds of ninety miles per hour or more. Though they will be extraordinarily long by the standards of today's cars and trucks, such vehicles will be articulated so as to be able to negotiate curves with ease. These vehicles will be powered by water, which, heated by burning some readily available fuel, will expand prodigiously as it un-

dergoes its metamorphosis from a liquid into a gas, creating almost unbelievable power that will drive even the largest engines. Driver error
will be nearly eliminated by placing the vehicles on fixed guideways or
"tracks."

The science of acoustics will be understood to such a thorough degree
that musical instruments will produce sound by purely mechanical
means, with no need for electrical amplification. One small instrument
with no electrical parts will be able to produce such a volume of sound
as to fill a large concert hall.

Universal musical education will eliminate the need for recorded music. Every family will own several musical instruments of the new mechanical sort, and each member will be able to perform competently on
at least one of them, providing the family with hours of wholesome
and improving entertainment.

Large openings covered with glass in the walls of office buildings will
virtually eliminate the need for artificial lighting during the day, as it
will be possible to harness the light of *the sun itself* for most everyday
tasks. A clever mechanical arrangement will make it possible to raise
the glass panels, allowing natural air circulation that will greatly re-
duce the need for artificial climate control.

The technique of acting will continue to improve. Actors will no longer
require multiple "takes" to act out a scene correctly, eliminating the
need to film their performances. Instead, audiences will gather in theaters to watch famous actors perform an entire movie in real time on a
specially constructed set that will take the place of the movie screen in

today's theaters.

Photography will no longer be bound by the limitations of digital tech-nology. Advances in chemistry will make it possible to record images directly on a specially prepared medium, which will be completely in-dependent of operating systems and changing fashions in digital stor-age. Different manufacturing processes will give these chemical media different characters, greatly enhancing the artistic possibilities inher-ent in photography.

"Good heavens, you're right. She *has* been drinking."

MEMORANDUM.

TO: All Employees
FROM: The President
SUBJECT: Quality Processes

My Fellow Employees:

All of us here at the Schenectady Small Arms & Biscuit Co. are doing our best to ensure that our work proceeds according to a quality
process that is measurable and accountable. Gone are the days when it
was enough to turn out a good, reliable product that people wanted to
buy—and good riddance, I say, to that benighted time. Today, in order to be competitive, we must manage our processes scientifically.
We must measure, measure, measure at every step of the way, and
only when our processes measure up to our numerical goals will we
have achieved true quality. The important thing to remember is that
the process is what we measure. It is not too much to say, in fact, that
the product itself is irrelevant. I myself have no idea what we manufacture these days.

It goes without saying, however, that a quality process is only as
good as the quality of the work put into it by quality team members. It
may be true that some of our quality processes are mildly cumber-
some, and that the maintenance of them consumes more than 50% of
the average working day; but you may be assured that these processes
have been established for good reasons, even if no one remembers

what the reasons are.

In regard to these processes, therefore, it is important to keep in mind that the quality of the process is only as good as the quality of the form by which it is measured. It has come to my attention that some team members have been filling out their Quality Process Tracking Sheets with irregular times, measuring the exact time it took them to complete a given task instead of filling in quarter-hour increments as it is clearly indicated on the form. Those quarter-hour increments are there for a reason, though it will do you no good to ask me what the reason was because the consultant who designed the forms is now living in Albuquerque under an assumed name. I probably should not have told you that. At any rate, the principle to remember is that, whatever task you need to accomplish, it must be made to fit the quarter-hour time increments on your Quality Process Tracking Sheet. In particular, I expect to see one quarter hour set aside for reading this memorandum on every single Quality Process Tracking Sheet turned in today.

Thank you very much for your prompt attention in this matter.

With Warmest Regards,
J. Rutherford Pinckney, President

NEW FALL LINEUP FROM DUMONT.

DISSATISFIED WITH THE ratings of its old new fall lineup, the Dumont Network has announced an entirely new new fall lineup, featuring several new one-hour dramatic series. "Diversity and variety," said Mr. Sid Pandarus, director of programming, "are the hallmarks of our new schedule." Among the new programs scheduled:

Walkies. When city police can't solve a case by themselves, they turn to Rosina Pym, whose extensive experience as a dog-walker to busy suburbanite families gives her a unique perspective on crime.

The Dadaist. When city police can't solve a case by themselves, they turn to Marcel de Ballon, a Dadaist poet who keeps babbling until he accidentally spews out the solution to the crime.

The Librarian. When city police can't solve a case by themselves, they turn to Miss Urquhart, whose intricate knowledge of the Dewey Decimal and Library of Congress cataloguing systems puts every form of information at her fingertips.

Mr. Fins. When city police can't solve a case by themselves, they rely on Mr. Fins, an Amazon River dolphin who lives at the city aquarium and solves crimes in his spare time.

The Detectives. When a group of amateur detectives from various disciplines can't solve a case by themselves, they dial 9-1-1 to summon the city police.

HAVE YOU EVER eaten too much of a delicious but unhealthy snack food? You may be entitled to compensation. Class-action lawsuit seeks to hold manufacturers responsible for the deliciousness of their snacks. Share your story with Lentill & Porridge, Attorneys at Law, Sheraden.

NO-FAULT IMPRIMATURS, nihil obstats, &c. Our staff of trained & fully qualified bishops is at your service 24 hours a day, 6 days a week. The Canon Law Practice of Rufinus & Rufinus, Troy Hill.

INSTRUCTIONS FOR OPERATING
THE PYRO-MATE WONDER MIDGET
HOME & OFFICE FIRE EXTINGUISHER.

1. ALWAYS call the fire department first. A fire, no matter how small, may spread out of your control more rapidly than you anticipate. A timely call to the fire department may spare you much disappointment later on in the process.

2. Once you have assured yourself that the fire department is on the way, retrieve the Pyro-Mate Wonder Midget Home & Office Fire Extinguisher from its handy Reddi-Stor wall-mounted storage bracket.

> A. First grasp the locking clasp firmly with the left hand, making sure to hold the locking tab between thumb and forefinger.

> B. Pull up and to the left.

> C. With the right hand, hold down the retainer arm, gripping it at a point approximately two-thirds of its length away from the left-hand end.

> D. Grasp the Pyro-Mate Wonder Midget Home &

Office Fire Extinguisher firmly in the left hand and pull it straight up. DO NOT release the retainer arm until the Pyro-Mate Wonder Midget Home & Office Fire Extinguisher is completely free of the Reddi-Stor wall-mounted storage bracket.

E. Return the retainer arm to its normal position until such time as it becomes necessary to replace the Pyro-Mate Wonder Midget Home & Office Fire Extinguisher in the Reddi Stor wall-mounted storage bracket.

3. Hold the Pyro-Mate Wonder Midget Home & Office Fire Extinguisher in an upright position. The words "Pyro-Mate Wonder Midget Home & Office Fire Extinguisher, Pyro-Mate Corp., Swissvale" should appear right-side-up on the right-hand side of the Pyro-Mate Wonder Midget Home & Office Fire Extinguisher. If the words "Pyro-Mate Wonder Midget Home & Office Fire Extinguisher, Pyro-Mate Corp., Swissvale" appear on the LEFT-hand side of the Pyro-Mate Wonder Midget Home & Office Fire Extinguisher, then the Pyro-Mate Wonder Midget Home & Office Fire Extinguisher is pointed toward you and will not extinguish the fire.

4. Carefully note the location of the fire. You may find that, by this time, the fire exists in more that one location.

5. Grasp the Insta-Lok locking pin firmly with the right hand and pull it straight toward you. Retain the Insta-Lok locking pin for future use: it will be necessary when returning the Pyro-Mate Wonder Midget

Home & Office Fire Extinguisher to its Reddi-Stor wall-mounted storage bracket.

6. Turn the arming lever approximately 75 degrees counter-clockwise to the "READY" position.

7. Remove the childproof cap from the Pyro-Mate Wonder Midget Home & Office Fire Extinguisher nozzle:

A. While pushing in firmly, squeeze the sides of the cap at the points marked S.

B. Turn the cap counter-clockwise until the triangular arrows on the cap and the body of the nozzle are aligned.

C. Push the cap away from the nozzle with both thumbs, placing one thumb on each side of the triangular arrow on the cap. Retain the cap for future use.

D. Remove the foil seal imprinted "SEALED FOR YOUR PROTECTION." If the seal is punctured or missing, DO NOT USE the Pyro-Mate Wonder Midget Home & Office Fire Extinguisher. Return the Pyro-Mate Wonder Midget Home & Office Fire Extinguisher to your Pyro-Mate dealer for a replacement.

8. Place the index finger of one hand firmly on the Power-Jet trigger,

using the other hand to support the weight of the Pyro-Mate Wonder Midget Home & Office Fire Extinguisher.

9. By this time the fire department should have arrived and extinguished the fire. Replace the childproof cap on the Pyro-Mate Wonder Midget Home & Office Fire Extinguisher nozzle.

10. Turn the arming lever approximately 75 degrees clockwise to the "NOT READY" position.

11. Carefully replace the Insta-Lok locking pin in its locking position.

12. Replace the Pyro-Mate Wonder Midget Home & Office Fire Extinguisher on the Reddi-Stor wall-mounted storage bracket, reversing steps A through D in section 2.

13. Since the seal is now broken on the nozzle of your Pyro-Mate Wonder Midget Home & Office Fire Extinguisher, contact your Pyro-Mate dealer immediately to order a new Pyro-Mate Wonder Midget Home & Office Fire Extinguisher.

CAPTAIN PLEONASM AND THE WORLD WITHOUT EVIL.

Although no recordings of the old Captain Pleonasm radio serial have survived, a number of the original scripts were recently unearthed in the archives of the Northern Broadcasting Company.

ANNOUNCER. Malt-O-Cod, the delicious and nutritious malt food drink flavored with real cod-liver oil, presents...

(Music: Theme, up and under for...)

ANNOUNCER. The Thrilling and Exciting Adventures of Captain Pleonasm and His Faithful and Trustworthy Sidekick and Assistant, Interjection Boy!

(Music: In full, then fade for...)

ANNOUNCER. As you recall, in last week's episode, Captain Pleonasm and Interjection Boy had defeated the combined forces of all the world's villains, forever ridding the world of evil and putting a stop to all bad things.

INTERJECTION BOY. Babblin' baboons, Captain Pleonasm! Have you got any threes?

CAPT. PLEONASM. It will be necessary for you to go fish. You will need to draw a card at random from the unsorted pile in the center of the table.

(*Music: Stinger.*)

INTERJECTION BOY. Golly golliwogs, Captain Pleonasm, you don't have to play that brassy dissonant chord every time you say that.

CAPT. PLEONASM. Have you any queens? Are there among your cards any portraits of—

INTERJECTION BOY. Merciful mockingbirds, Captain Pleonasm, you can just say it once. I got the idea the first time. Go fish.

CAPT. PLEONASM. Ah. I must draw a card from the irregular mass of cards before me. It is necessary, for the further progress of the game, that I should take—

INTERJECTION BOY. Good grief, will you just take a card?

CAPT. PLEONASM. Aha! I have drawn a queen from the pile! Completely at random, with no foreknowledge of the card toward which my fingers were moving, I have nevertheless taken out exactly the card that was required for my ultimate victory!

(*Music: Stinger.*)

INTERJECTION BOY. Gee whiz, you can be annoying sometimes.

CAPT. PLEONASM. And now it is once again my turn. My withdrawal of the precise card for which I had asked has entitled me to ask you for another card. Have you any kings? Among your cards, are—

INTERJECTION BOY. Go fish, for Pete's sake.

CAPT. PLEONASM. Hmmm. It was not a king. I shall not reveal to you the exact card which I have withdrawn, but I must regretfully inform you that it was not the card for which I had asked.

INTERJECTION BOY. Yeah, whatever. Have you got any sevens?

CAPT. PLEONASM. By "sevens," do you mean cards with that precise number of figures or symbols? Would the Arabic numeral seven appear in the corner? And does it matter precisely what the figures are? Is there any particular figure you—

INTERJECTION BOY. Holy Sandusky, Captain Pleonasm, you've got three of them, haven't you?

CAPT. PLEONASM. Well, I cannot tell a lie. To prevaricate is contrary to my nature. It would go against every principle for which I have stood in the fight against evil were I to deny what is literally true.

INTERJECTION BOY. Indignant iguanas, Captain Pleonasm! I'm getting tired of this game.

CAPT. PLEONASM. Are you indeed? Well, then, there is one thing

I have saved for just such an occasion. It is something so exciting, so pulse-quickening in fact, that I have held it in reserve, knowing that a time might come when we required more spiritual stimulation, more heart-pounding appeal to the adrenal glands, than the ordinary pastimes in which we have hitherto indulged can provide.

INTERJECTION BOY. Great   tumbling   redwoods,   Captain Pleonasm! What is it?

CAPT. PLEONASM. Charades!

(*Music: Stinger.*)

INTERJECTION BOY. Heavens to Betsy, Captain Pleonasm, is it too late to un-defeat some of those villains?

ANNOUNCER. Will a rousing game of charades provide the excitement Interjection Boy longs for? Will Captain Pleonasm have to haul out the Parcheesi game he keeps under the bed? Will Interjection Boy accidentally leave the gate unlocked at the maximum-security prison? Don't miss next week's enthralling and riveting episode of the Thrilling and Exciting Adventures of Captain Pleonasm and His Faithful and Trustworthy Sidekick and Assistant, Interjection Boy!

(*Music: Theme, in full and under for...*)

ANNOUNCER. When Captain Pleonasm is feeling oppressed by the ennui of modern existence, what always perks him up? It's Malt-O-Cod, the only malt beverage flavored with 100% real cod-liver oil.

Kids, ask your moms for Malt-O-Cod, now with an official Captain Pleonasm Old Maid deck in every package. It's the malt food drink that's brain food—Malt-O-Cod.

(*Music: In full, then out.*)

IMPROVED DECIMAL CLOCKS in the latest styles. Tell time the rational way. Ask about our new 1,000-day One-Year Kilocalendar. Rationalistic Chronometer Corp., Fairywood.

PLODLEIGH'S ANCIENT MYSTERIES.

Program 17: Warriors of the Cliffs.

WELCOME TO Plodleigh's Ancient Mysteries. I'm Kenny
Plodleigh, and tonight we explore the mysterious rise and even more
mysterious disappearance of one of the greatest forgotten cultures in
the world: the ruthless but highly civilized, um, uh—oh, it's just on
the tip of my tongue... It began with a C, or a CH sound, like
"Chimichanga" or something, except that's what I had for dinner last
night. But it was something like that. It sounded a lot like that, except
of course it wasn't. Chipotle, that's it. No, wait. Well, that's ridiculous. I mean, I've spent months studying these people, and I can't remember their name. Here I am standing in the middle of the ruins of
Whatchamacallit, the ancient capital and fortress of this forgotten civilization, and I have absolutely no idea what I'm supposed to call them.
Chiclets, Chillingsworths, Chichesters, Tschaikowskies, something
that starts with a CH. I was going to tell you all about how they suddenly rose to power in the thirteenth century and conquered a small
empire in the Andes, but it's not much of a story if I keep having to
call them the Thingummies all the way through, is it? Or maybe it was
the eleventh century. If it's the twelve hundreds, is that the thirteenth
century or the eleventh? I always get that mixed up. I know it's not
the twelfth, because that would be too easy. Let's see, we're in the
twenty-first century now, and it's the two thousands, so, um, if I sub-

tract, and carry the nineteen, it comes out to, so it is the eleventh after all. And that was when these Whosits built this vast fortress complex you see behind me, but they didn't have a written language, you see, so it's not as though they could just spray-paint their name over the gate where I could read it to you. And then I would have been rappelling into that dark hole over there where there's evidence that the Whaddayacallems made human sacrifices of warriors from their traditional enemies, the Thingies. Well, a fine scene that's going to make now. I can just see me dangling from a rope in the dark, talking about the Whoevers defeating the Whatstheirnames. I might as well just call it quits and fill up the rest of the hour with reruns of My Mother the Car for all the good I'm doing here. I think I'll go back to my comfortable hotel room, where it doesn't smell so much like hot llamas and I can get a nice cup of tea, and maybe it will come to me there.

Program 35: The Counter-Mound Builders.

WELCOME ONCE AGAIN to Plodleigh's Ancient Mysteries. I'm Kenny Plodleigh, and tonight we explore the mysterious Mon Valley Culture, whose once-powerful empire stretched from present-day Munhall all the way up to present-day Monessen or thereabouts. When other North American cultures were building mounds, this extraordinary people were building inverse mounds, known to archaeologists as holes. In fact, current archaeological research indicates that the raw materials for the mounds in the Hopewell Culture may have come from the holes created by the sophisticated Mon Valley Culture, which is indeed an extraordinary example of intercultural cooperation.

Now, I was going to take you on a tour of the most spectacular Mon Valley Culture site, the Duquesne Ditch, but the Duquesne city police, whose name is Harold, informed us that we needed a permit to film at the site. So we went to the next-most-famous Mon Valley Culture site, the West Elizabeth Hole-in-the-Ground, but someone had built a Uni-Mart on top of it. So I drew a diagram of one of these Mon Valley inverse mounds on this cocktail napkin I picked up at Motzsky's in New Eagle. And as you can see, it starts out level like this, then goes down quite a bit, and then comes back up on the other side, and it's level again over here. This extraordinary design is repeated over and over again in the various Mon Valley Culture inverse mounds. What is even more extraordinary is that these remarkable architects, whom we once thought of as primitive savages, had the technology to dig through solid asphalt or even concrete, to judge by the large number of inverse mounds found today in asphalt and concrete pavements throughout the Mon Valley area. Here's another cocktail napkin showing how we think they did it. This figure here, with the happy face, is using a primitive jackhammer fashioned from flint and old shower-curtain rods, all bound together with dental floss. He has a happy face because he's hammering right through the concrete, leaving a big inverse mound right in the middle of the pavement. This stick right here is his arm, because I can't draw arms very well. He probably has two arms, but I only drew one of them. And this mean-looking thing over here with the fangs is Harold, the Duquesne cop, who's saying in this talk balloon, "Do you have a permit for that?" Ha ha—it's a sort of joke, you see. And that's how we think the Mon Valley Culture made the many inverse mounds we see all over the Mon Valley today. Well, that's all we have for this week, because I'm out of cocktail napkins, so until next week, this is Kenny Plodleigh wishing you all kinds of great adventures. Join us next week when we explore the mysterious parallel stripes that sometimes cover acres of asphalt around shopping centers in suburban Robinson Township.

Program 43: Mall Builders of the Monongahela.

KENNY PLODLEIGH HERE with another edition of *Plodleigh's Ancient Mysteries.* Today we venture once again into the ancient and mysterious valley of the Monongahela, a landscape littered with the remains of lost civilizations.

These magnificent ruins behind me, still impressive after literally decades, once formed one of the most remarkable constructions of the remarkably advanced peoples who inhabited this storied valley. We know from their ancient writings that these people called this palatial structure a "mall," but as yet there is no agreement among archaeologists as to what its purpose might have been.

Some believe that it may have been a vast religious complex, perhaps housing hundreds of monks dedicated to the service of the gods Gimbels and J. C. Penney, the names you can still see in faded letters at opposite ends of the structure.

Others suggest that it may have been the palace of a powerful chieftain, whose many retainers occupied the numerous large cells arranged along a corridor between the two large throne-rooms; on this hypothesis, Gimbels and J. C. Penney may have been the names of the chieftain and his queen.

But I think the most plausible hypothesis is that the whole complex was a sort of primitive Internet, where goods of all descriptions could be purchased. According to this view, each of the stalls along the central corridor would have been a separate Web site dealing in a particular specialty, while the magnificent chambers at the ends were mega-sites, similar to our Amazon.com, in which a wide variety of merchandise might be procured. This hypothesis has the advantage of solving the longstanding mystery of how primitive peoples carried on commerce on a large scale before the introduction of even a rudimentary form of hypertext transfer protocol.

I wish I could show you how magnificently preserved the interior is, but our insurance company won't let us take the cameras in there. So join us next week, when we'll be exploring the world of chivalry and romance as we delve deep into the secrets of the Knights of Colum-bus. Until then, I'm Kenny Plodleigh for *Plodleigh's Ancient Mysteries*, and after that I'll probably still be Kenny Plodleigh. There—you told me to put some jokes in, so was that funny enough?

THE ASP'S ARIA.

It was not generally made public until recently that the libretto to Heyser's well-received new opera, The Death of Cleopatra, was written by the eminent novelist and poet Irving Vanderblock-Wheedle. The Asp's Aria, sung by Julietta della Fripperia to Heyser's haunting cacophony of bassoons and kazoos, has been singled out for especial praise.

[*Lento arigato.*]

Excuse me, please, but did I overhear
A queen's lament, with many a bitter tear?
You'll find a true friend lurking very near:
I am (and please try not to gasp)
An asp.

Has it occurred to you what quick relief
Would comfort you and silence all your grief—
How short your cares would be, your tears how brief,
If to your bosom you should clasp
An asp?

I happen to have made my little nest
Right here, in this bejeweled little chest
(For you'll agree that little chests are best):

Now just pull out the bolt and grasp
The hasp.

I'll be your passp-
Ort to eternity and lasting fame:
Soon girls from Glassp-
Ort to Sewickley will usurp your name,
If you will lift the hasp
And just reach in and grasp
And to your bosom clasp
(Forgive my vocal rasp)
An asp.

PRACTICAL STANDARD LETTER-WRITER.

OUR YOUNG PEOPLE are writing with greater enthusiasm and fre-quency than ever before, largely because of the prevalence of text messaging in the youth culture of today. Yet the abysmal literary qual-ity of these communications has often been remarked. Dr. Boli is of the opinion that this deficiency is to be attributed to the lack of good models, such as were readily available when he was a young man in the form of "standard letter-writers," collections of letters for every common circumstance. In this occasional series, Dr. Boli attempts to fill that gap by providing useful examples to show how the art of text messaging might be raised to a higher standard.

A Young Gentleman at School,
Thanking His Mother for a Packaged Luncheon.

My dearest mother,

Though I needed no token to recall you to memory, and indeed it would be impossible that any material demonstration of your affection could cause me to hold you in more sincere esteem than I do already, yet the excellent luncheon of which I have even now only just com-pleted the consumption, and which was as delightful to the gustatory and olfactory senses as it was nourishing, has occasioned me to dwell with even greater earnestness on all your past favors, and to marvel once again at your ceaseless attention to my comfort and happiness. I may tell you in confidence that the luncheons you provide me, which by their very appearance testify to the many minutes of loving care you have lavished on their preparation, have aroused no little envy among the other students in (Mr./Ms./Miss/Mrs.) (name of teacher)'s kindergarten class; but I am happy to say that the good nature of the children, and the patient but firm leadership of their teacher, have prevailed, and that their envy has expressed itself rather in friendly congratulations to me than in any of those unbecoming species of behavior that so marred my otherwise enjoyable experience of nursery school last year. I am sure I need not tell you how grateful I feel for this fresh mark of your maternal devotion, as I trust you will give me credit for those filial feelings which are appropriate to a boy who has received such a singular demonstration of his beloved parent's affection.

As for myself, and what has happened to me since I departed from you at the bus stop this morning, I have little to report. I continue to enjoy excellent health, and nothing has occurred to cast a cloud over my general happiness, so that I am confident of meeting you this afternoon in a state of good cheer appropriate to one who has received far more than he can ever hope to repay from his beloved mother. With my best duty to my father, believe me,

My dear mother,
your ever dutiful and obliged son,
[Name].

Letter from a Young Gentleman
to a Prospective Employer.

Dear Sir:

It is, as I have always believed, incumbent upon every young man who is reasonably healthy, and of sound mental capacity, to seek by any means to render himself useful to the world at large, and to exercise his God-given abilities in a manner that conduces at once to the benefit of his community and to his own development, both in skill and in virtue. It behooves him, in fact, to be always "on the lookout," to use a colorful colloquial expression, for any such opportunity; nor should he allow one to pass when it presents itself.

This is my excuse for imposing upon your attention at the present moment: for after last night's considerable accumulation of snow, I made a brief survey of our street, and happened to notice (I hope you will pardon the liberty) that your sidewalk had not yet been cleared of that attractive but inconvenient crystalline deposit which nature, in her bounty, shed so abundantly but indiscriminately over our neighborhood.

Here at once I perceived a chance both to render a valuable service and to put my otherwise idle hands (for you must be aware that city schools are closed today) to good use. In short, for I would not waste your time unnecessarily, I thought that I might undertake the removal of the snow from your sidewalk.

It is customary on such occasions for the owner of the property to offer a small remuneration; the generally accepted rate at present is ten dollars an hour. I believe the entire job could be completed in one hour, in addition, of course, to the three hours I have spent composing this message, for a total of only $40, exclusive of applicable taxes. Hoping, therefore, to receive a favorable response at your earliest convenience, I am

Your ready and obedient servant,
[Name].

Letter from a Gentleman to a Lady,
disclosing his passion.

Madam,

It cannot have escaped your notice that the considerable merits of your person and conversation have attracted my attention, and indeed on more than one occasion I have ventured to speak with you, however briefly. Having been moderately pleased by these encounters, I have resolved to declare my sentiments of affection for you, confident that in doing so I am making a rational decision that is reasonably likely to redound to the happiness of both of us.

You will doubtless be happy to know that I have done my "due diligence," as the lawyers say, and have not entered into this enterprise lightly. When my attention was first attracted in your direction, I took some care to ascertain that you were indeed the sort of young lady to whom it would be suitable to pay such respects as I now express to you. For the preliminary survey, I was fortunate to be able to rely on the assistance of an acquaintance who is employed by the Federal Bureau of Investigation, and please let me be the first to say that I find nothing unforgivable in your negligible criminal record. Judging by the police reports, I do believe that hot-dog vendor had it coming to him.

Having made these brief investigations, I determined to find out whether you were indeed the sort of person with whom it might be tolerable to share a household. It was, of course, essential that you should not observe me as I made my own observations, so that your behavior should be as natural and unaffected as possible. For this purpose the maple trees that give your house such delightful shade in summer proved eminently suitable. After weeks of observation, I determined that you had a charming way of attacking a grapefruit, that you did not leave the sink a revolting mess after brushing your teeth, and that you cheated only moderately on your income tax. In short, my judgment was on balance favorable to you.

Trusting, therefore, that you will grant me a favorable reply at your earliest convenience, I now sign myself,

Your affectionate admirer and sincere friend,

[Name.]

"That does it! If they're going to make that ruckus every night, I'm going to take up the sousaphone."

THE FREE MAN.

*From Dr. Boli's Fables for Children
Who Are Too Old to Believe in Fables.*

ONCE A LITTLE girl was walking along in the cheerful summer forest when she came across a man who was tied to a tree by every sort of
chain and shackle.

"Oh, you poor prisoner!" the little girl exclaimed. "I'll run and get
help for you immediately!"

"No, no, you misunderstand," said the man, who was bound but not
gagged, so that at least he could say anything he liked. "I am a completely free man."

"You don't look free to me," said the little girl. "For one thing,
you're chained to the tree by that thing around your waist."

"Oh, I put that chain there," the man explained. "I wanted to be
safe from falling down, so I chained myself to this tree, which as you
can see is quite sturdy. This way I'll never fall down and bump my
head. No price is too high for security, you know."

"But your legs are shackled together," the little girl remarked.

"You're very observant," the man answered. "If my legs could
move freely, they might slide apart, and I would start to slip down the
tree, which would be very uncomfortable. So you see, since I've
chained myself to the tree, it's much more comfortable to have my
legs shackled."

"But your right arm is chained to this big branch with a bronze chain," the little girl said.

"It's gold," the man replied.

"It looks like bronze to me," the little girl said.

"I was assured that it was gold," the man told her. "A very rich man came along with this beautiful gold chain and told me that, if I would let him chain my right arm with it, then I could admire his gold chain all the time, and I would never have to stop looking at it."

"But your left hand is tied to the chain behind your back," the little girl said.

"Yes," the man agreed. "You see, I'm right-handed, so it's not much use to me to have my left hand flailing about, is it?"

"I see," the little girl said. "And you're sure you don't want me to go find someone to untie you?"

"Oh, no," said the man. "I have chosen every one of my chains and shackles with absolute freedom. There is not a man on earth who is freer than I."

So the little girl told the man that it had been pleasant talking with him, and the man wished her a very good day, and the little girl went on her way into the lovely green forest, thinking about what she had seen and heard.

"Well," the little girl said to herself as she walked, "I suppose he seems happy enough. But still, I'm glad I'm not free. I don't think I'd like it at all."

COMING SOON TO A THEATER NEAR YOU.

She Said She Loved Me. A romantic comedy in which a man and a woman who initially hate each other begin to discover that they're falling in love. But will their budding romance survive the ninjas who suddenly show up at the 58-minute mark?

Indians & Indians. A Hindu immigrant village in the Old West is menaced by hostile tribes. Meanwhile, half a world away, Native American students at a culinary school in colonial Bombay are menaced by Hindu fundamentalists. Also, for some reason, there are ninjas.

Spare. Can a bowling team filled with comical losers and misfits defeat a gang of ninjas terrorizing the bowling alleys of Camden?

The Ninja. A young man's accidental exposure to radioactive waste gives him the fabled powers of the ninja, but since he's already a trained ninja he really doesn't notice the difference.

THE TELEPHONE.

From the Notebooks of Irving Vanderblock-Wheedle, Undated.

The telephone: it rings, and when I answer,
Stark silence reigns: a silence like the grave—
An empty grave, with no dead person in it,
So that not even sounds of rotting flesh,
Weak as they are, disturb the lifeless hush,
The quiet of a grim eternity
Of emptiness—and I stand on the edge
Of the abyss, still bellowing my greeting
Into the boundless blackness of the depths,
Where it is swallowed up in nothingness.
But just before I utterly despair,
Light dawns, and hope returns: the universe
Basks in the glow of life: my empty ear
Fills up, and I hear sound—O blessed sound!—
A voice—a human voice—from Bangalore.

From the PREFACE
to the *Shorter History of the United States*,
by Irving Vanderblock-Wheedle.

IT IS CUSTOMARY when placing before the public the fruits of
one's labors to begin by offering some apology or explanation for the
work, especially when the field is crowded with similar offerings. In
this case, however, no such apology is necessary. Although more than
one history of the United States may be found on library shelves, and
perhaps even not a few making some claim to brevity, the neglect in
such productions of the manifold contributions of Mr. William Rufus
DeVane King has become a byword among serious students of history.
The snobbish elitism of professional historians is the only conceivable
explanation for this scandalous omission, for among the common people the memory of King shines bright, as the numerous cycles of popular legends and ballads about him testify:

"Mr. William Rufus DeVane King was Vice-President
Of the United States when in Cuba he was resident,"

runs one jump-rope rhyme still heard in schoolyards across the nation.
But there is no need to elaborate this point: we all remember the songs
and stories from our school days, and the very land around us is littered with evidences of the popular devotion to the memory of this
great American. King Street in Alexandria—King George Street in

Annapolis (named for King and some man called George, otherwise lost to history)—the designation of Brooklyn as King's County—all these and countless other tributes may be found scattered across the map by anyone with the ambition to consult an atlas.

Why, then, the notorious neglect of the man and his accomplishments in our standard histories? As we said, the explanation can only be snobbishness; but to what do we owe this peculiar outbreak of that literary disease?

Part of the answer may be found in political prejudice. William Rufus DeVane King was one of the founders of the state of Alabama; but no reasonable observer could hold him entirely responsible for that, since he could not possibly have foreseen the Alabama of today. There is also the matter of his name, of which there seems to be entirely too much, and perhaps historians have been reluctant to bulk up their productions with repeated references to William Rufus DeVane King when the same number of pages could hold many more years of history involving lesser figures with more economical names, such as John Adams. Andrew Jackson, who was noted for his urbane wit, referred to our subject as "Miss Nancy," and if the name had stuck, we historians might have been spared a great deal of scribbling.

Finally, there is the embarrassing question of slavery. William Rufus DeVane King was one of the largest slaveholders in the South (measured, that is, by number of slaves; the man himself was rather petite), and this fact may have deterred some historians from addressing his other accomplishments. With these reservations we have considerable sympathy. In the present work, we have adopted the attitude of the recent revision of *Huckleberry Finn*, and have decided to address the issue of William Rufus DeVane King's slave ownership by pretending that he kept Yorkshire terriers instead.

"EYEBALL" PORTION SIZES.

YOU CAN AVOID the pointless drudgery of weighing everything you eat by comparing portions to common household objects.

Cheese: One ping-pong ball

Sauerkraut: Half a golf club

Water: A small fax machine

Spinach: The carburetor of a 1934 DeSoto Airflow

Butter: One lump of butter

Beef: 1/482 of a cow

Pasta (cooked): A stapler

Fruit Jelly: One of the fruit from which it is made, minus a gross of "falcon" steel pens

Dinner Roll: One dinner roll

Fish: One volume of the 1834 edition of Isaac Disraeli's *Curiosities of Literature*

Potato: One hamburger

UNPLUGGED.

ARE YOU LOOKING for wholesome activities for the whole family to enjoy away from the television, computer, tablet, or electric toaster? Here are a few suggestions for things to do while you're unplugged:

Write an epic. Choose a historical subject with a broad sweep, such as your town's incorporation as a borough.

Dig a hole. Everyone loves to dig, and holes have many practical uses in the garden or parlor.

Teach yourself abstract expressionism. It's easier than you might think.

Move a piano. For their size, pianos are heavier than any other object you will find in the house. The logistics of moving one even just between rooms will keep you entertained for hours.

Start a political party. Most successful political parties were started by bored people with too much time on their hands.

Mow the lawn. Do you remember whether you have a lawn? Try looking outside. If you have no lawn, perhaps you have a shag rug, which can be just as much fun.

Build your own Ponzi scheme. Ponzi schemes are lots of fun, and the best part is that even the wealthiest investors will fall for them if you tell a good story.

Mope. Moping can consume hours or even days and requires no other equipment than an active imagination.

Count your fingers and toes. You may think you know the answer already, but when was the last time you actually tried the experiment?

HOW TO KEEP FIT.

KEEP THE TEAPOT on the other side of the room.

Instead of making a left turn, make three right turns. You will burn three times the calories turning the steering wheel, to say nothing of applying pressure to the brake and accelerator alternately.

If your office is on the third floor, instead of taking the elevator all the way up, change elevators on the second floor.

Sneeze. Sneezing uses many otherwise idle muscles in the upper body. Alternate hands when you cover your mouth, so as to exercise your arms evenly.

Prefer comedies to dramas on television. Laughing uses many of the same muscles exercised by sneezing.

Instead of large chips, eat chips of the smallest size you can find, and eat them one at a time. You will raise your hand to your mouth two or three times as often, burning calories each time. Popcorn is an excellent snack for this sort of exercise.

Train your dog to be in the way, so as to prevent walking from one place to another in a straight line. This is one of the easiest tasks for a dog to learn.

Yell a lot. Yelling burns much more energy than ordinary talking.

Find a popular text on ergonomics that shows how to arrange your workspace to make everything you do as easy and efficient as possible. Then do the opposite of what the book says.

THOMAS ALVA EDISON didn't like zucchini. Send $15 in unmarked bills for details.

THE LONG DAY.

N.B.—Dr. Boli has designed this story for beginning readers. It uses a limited, but unpredictable, vocabulary, and is well suited to early reading lessons.

A man and a cat sat on the grass.

"It is a hot day," said the cat.

"No, it is cold," said the man.

"I say it is hot," said the cat.

"I say it is cold," said the man.

"Let us ask the dog," said the cat.

So they asked the dog, "Is it a hot day or a cold day?"

The dog said, "It is a red day."

"I say it is hot," said the cat.

"I say it is cold," said the man.

"I say it is red," said the dog.

"Let us ask the cow," said the cat.

So they asked the cow, "Is it a hot day, or a cold day, or a red day?"

The cow said, "It is a sharp day."

"I say it is hot," said the cat.

"I say it is cold," said the man.

"I say it is red," said the dog.

"I say it is sharp," said the cow.

"Let us ask the sheep," said the cat.

So they asked the sheep, "Is it a hot day, or a cold day, or a red day, or a sharp day?"

The sheep said, "It is a round day."

"I say it is hot," said the cat.

"I say it is cold," said the man.

"I say it is red," said the dog.

"I say it is sharp," said the cow.

"I say it is round," said the sheep.

"Let us ask the goat," said the cat.

So they asked the goat, "Is it a hot day, or a cold day, or a red day, or a sharp day, or a round day?"

The goat said, "It is a thick day."

"I say it is hot," said the cat.

"I say it is cold," said the man.

"I say it is red," said the dog.

"I say it is sharp," said the cow.

"I say it is round," said the sheep.

"I say it is thick," said the goat.

"Let us ask the hen," said the cat.

So they asked the hen, "Is it a hot day, or a cold day, or a red day, or a sharp day, or a round day, or a thick day?"

The hen said, "It is not a hot day, or a cold day, or a red day, or a sharp day, or a round day, or a thick day. It is not a day at all. Now it is night, and it is time to go to sleep."

FASHION HINTS.

IT IS CONSIDERED bad form to wear a baseball cap to a funeral unless the deceased is also wearing a baseball cap. Check with relatives before the ceremony.

Mao suits are "in" this fall.

Ladies may obtain the effect of fashionable high-heeled shoes without the inconvenience by means of a judicious use of trompe-l'oeil painting.

If you are a classical musician, remember that the same dress that wins applause at the symphony can get you arrested for soliciting three blocks away.

Before you wear a T-shirt with the logo of a heavy-metal band on it to church, check on line to see whether the band is embarrassingly passé.

If you are considering a tattoo, make sure to remind the artist that you want a design that expresses your own irreducible individuality. Then pick the same tattoo all the other cool kids are getting.

Labor Day is coming up soon, so remember to burn your white shoes, or drop them off at a local public incinerator station.

ORIGINS OF POPULAR WEDDING CUSTOMS.

The wedding ring. An ancient Germanic superstition, older than recorded history, held that a bride's finger would fall off on the wedding night if not bound with iron. Gold or silver is now usually substituted for the traditional iron, but the meaning of the gesture is the same.

Throwing shoes. In the days when brides were commonly obtained by abduction from neighboring tribes, it was natural for the relatives of the bride to make use of whatever projectiles came to hand, or to foot, if one may use the expression.

Bridesmaids. These were originally members of the bride's bodyguard, and still retain the custom of dressing in uniform.

Throwing the garter. Originally the garter held a concealed dagger; with the disappearance of that traditional accessory, the garter itself had to be thrown, and the supposed meaning of the tradition underwent a subtle change.

Tossing rice. Rice began to be substituted in the nineteenth century for the more traditional, but more expensive, buckshot.

Honeymoon. The wedding trip or honeymoon vacation originated in the custom of running like blazes as far as possible away from the angry mob of the bride's relatives.

HEALTH AT HOME. Let's face it: licensed chiropractors are expensive. But now you can cut out the middleman with our new Home Chiropractic Center. This all-in-one steam-powered unit requires only water and a generous supply of coal. Not responsible for injuries.

LAST WORDS OF NOTABLE FIGURES.

"Don't publish it till you've livened it up with some jokes." —Thomas Aquinas, author of the *Summa Theologica*.

"Because I could not stop for death,
He kindly stopped for me,
And something something tumty tum,
I'll fill the rest in later." —Emily Dickinson, poet.

"I showed them, didn't I?" —Richard M. Nixon, former president.

"Don't forget to put the cat out. She has been on fire for some time now." —Samuel Johnson, lexicographer.

"What, you didn't like cake?" —Marie Antoinette, queen of France.

"I wonder why they call this a keystone." —Magnus Schiff, founder, Schiff Demolition Services, Inc.

"I'd like a second opinion." —Samuel Hahnemann, discoverer of homeopathy.

"I have a speech for this melancholy occasion that I have been preparing for more than forty years. It goes like this." —Daniel Webster, senator.

DEVIL KING KUN.

Chapter One.

I WAS SITTING up reading late one evening, at the end of what I may truly call in hindsight the last ordinary day of my existence, when my man Banks came padding into the room.

"Excuse me, sir. A gentleman to see you."

At that moment the clock beside me struck eleven—the last hour I would ever hear it strike.

"Who would be calling at this hour?" I asked. "Well, show him in."

But that proved unnecessary, as the gentleman in question appeared in the doorway, pushing his way past Banks, who shrugged and padded off into the pantry. It was my old friend and former colleague Norbert Weyland—the square, resolute jaw and piercing blue eyes were unmistakable.

"Good old Peevish!" he greeted me cheerfully, turning out the overhead light. "Didn't expect me at this hour, did you?" He yanked the desk lamp out of its socket. "In fact, didn't expect me back from Tierra del Fuego at all, I'll wager. How are you, old boy?" He stepped into the bathroom for a moment and flushed the night light down the toilet. "You look fit and happy, or at least you did when I could see you. Now, bolt all your doors, lock your windows, nail the cat flap shut, push heavy furniture in front of the vents, stop all your drains, stack telephone books on the toilet lid, and put child safety covers on all your electrical outlets. There. Expeditiously done, old boy, especially in the dark. Now write a note to whom it may concern saying that you've moved to Kansas City and taken a job selling beets from a cart with no fixed address. Splendid. I always could rely on you to take directions. And now, I expect you're wondering what all this is about."

"A little," I admitted.

In the dim illumination from the streetlights outside, I could see his silhouette: he was peering intently through the window. "Fact is, I've come here on the trail of an archfiend."

"A what?"

"An archfiend. It's a bit like an archbishop, but fiendier. Anyway, that's why I came back from Tierra del Fuego, by way of Sao Paolo, Chittagong, Lagos, Tristan da Cunha, and Monroeville, following his fiendish trail. But now it looks as though the wily devil is on my trail instead. If we're lucky, I gave him the slip on my way here. If we're not—well..."

"But who is this fiend? It's not like you to be rattled like this."

"He has many names," Weyland said softly. "Irving Spatz, for one. Alias Manuel Ormsby, alias Rudolphus Cramm, alias Jimmy Smatter the Dancing Barber of the Boulevard of the Allies, alias President James Buchanan, alias Sir George Pickerel-Farmington, alias Blanche 'Boom Boom' Helmholtz, alias Weng Fao of the Sûreté, alias the Great Blando; but he is known to his legions of fanatical followers as Kun, the devil king."

"Why would they follow someone they think of as the devil?"

"He gives them free beer. Do you see the fiendishly intricate brilliance of the man's mind?"

He turned to face me, or at least it sounded as though he was facing me now. "Peevish, old man, you need to know the facts. I don't think I'm exaggerating when I say the future of our race depends on my success."

"What race is that?" I asked, rather stupidly I fear.

"The African, North and South American, Asian, Australian, European, and Oceanian race. In other words, the non-Andorran race."

"Well, that's a strange way of putting it."

"Not if you know Kun, the devil king. He has sworn destruction or slavery to all non-Andorrans. In his mind, he is the messiah of the Andorran race, a race peculiarly formed of two of the great conquering peoples of the world, and a race as it were distilled and epitomized in himself. His keen Andorran brain combines all the Spanish passion and Jesuitical intellectual precision with all the French dexterity with sauces. He knows that the eighty-five thousand restless Andorrans only await their leader, and he knows that they will be invincible with him at their head.

"But what kind of name is Kun for a man from Andorra? It doesn't sound Catalan, or French or Spanish for that matter."

"We think it's an acronym."

"An acronym? But an acronym for what?"

"Ah, Peevish, old boy, if we knew that!"

"And you say this Kun means to enslave us all?" I still found it difficult to believe that such evil could exist in the world.

"Yes, and I have good reason to believe I know where he intends to start. And that's why I have to warn the archbishop."

"Who?"

"The archbishop. He's like an archfiend, but on our side. And that's where you come in, Peevish, old man. We'll be needing your car.

That, in fact, is why I came to you. No one else drives a car as blandly inconspicuous as yours. It is positively the only vehicle in which we have any chance of reaching our destination."

"I'll have Banks bring it round," I told Weyland; and I immediately rang for Banks.

When I received no reply after half a minute, I rang again. There was still no reply.

I called out. "Banks! Banks, stop lallygagging about and get the car ready!"

Suddenly I felt a hand grip my arm. "Peevish!" Weyland whispered. "Where did you leave Banks?"

"Last time I saw, he was headed for the pantry."

"Where is the pantry?"

"It's just back there, through the library and the music room, down the hall past the conservatory and through the dining room. You can't miss it. It's a small apartment, after all."

"Lead the way. I fear the worst."

I led him through the darkened apartment until at last we reached the pantry, which I announced by saying, "This is the pantry."

"Put on the light," he said.

I did.

The scene of horror that met my eyes was so unexpected that at first I could not parse it at all. Banks was there on the floor; or, rather, his legs were there. The rest of him was completely obscured by a gigan- tic anvil that had evidently been dropped on him from the ceiling. Some of the hoisting tackle was still scattered about the pantry.

"The fiend!" Weyland whispered, with a peculiar combination of frustration and disgust. "I should have known! He got Sir Gregory Pramwheeler the same way."

"But how did he get an anvil into my apartment? And how did he hoist it and drop it without our hearing it?"

"You see now what we're up against," Weyland replied grimly.

This story will be continued only if there is sufficient interest. By "interest," of course, Dr. Boli means his own, not yours.

SETTLERS WANTED

THE WIDE OPEN spaces of West Mifflin are yours for the taking, if you are willing to put your back into it and fend off the natives. Free pamphlets show you how to chop down a typical suburban split-level and use the material to build a comfortable wigwam.

" 'Lutheran' my eye! You didn't tell me you were
from that d——d Wisconsin Synod!" (Page 1443.)

MEMORANDUM.

TO: All Employees
FROM: The President
RE: Current Economic Conditions

My Fellow Employees:

All of us here at the Schenectady Small Arms & Biscuit Co., and I include myself in that number, have been aware for some time of the effects of the current economic slowdown. Certain painful decisions are facing us, and I must confess that my own position is not one to be envied. There are times when I wish with all my heart that I could be a simple cog in the machine, like all of you, instead of the leader to whom hundreds of employees look for inspiration.

For the past two years, our Mr. Ernest Poplar, Director of the Investments Department, has been warning senior executives, including myself, that certain investments in which we had placed the Company's funds were not sound. With simple but elegant mathematical reasoning, he and his senior staff demonstrated that it was not possible for the funds in which we had invested to maintain the rate of return they had maintained unless some sort of fraud was at work.

Unfortunately, executives, including myself, were more persuaded by the arguments of Mr. Reginald Gull, our Chief Financial Officer, who reasoned that the concept of "soundness" was an outdated notion in what he called the age of postmodern investment. Basing our decisions on Mr. Gull's advice, we placed much of the Company's assets in a small number of funds which have now been revealed to be nothing less than "Fonzie schemes," as I believe Mr. Poplar calls them. Although we are taking all possible steps to recover at least our initial investment, practically speaking we must regard that money as lost.

It is never an easy thing for me to announce layoffs, but painful realities dictate a tightening of the belt. A certain number of staff reductions must be made in order to keep our expenditures within our means.

It is therefore my difficult duty to announce that Mr. Ernest Poplar and his senior staff will no longer be employed by the Schenectady Small Arms & Biscuit Co., and that all remaining employees in the Investments Department will be transferred to the direct supervision of Mr. Reginald Gull, our Chief Financial Officer. Mr. Poplar has already been escorted from the building. In answer to some of your questions, the duct tape was only to prevent Mr. Poplar from injuring himself, as there was some fear that he might be subject to seizures.

A special notice to remaining senior executives: please stop by my office to pick up your bonus checks, which you have more than earned by facing the trauma of belt-tightening with a stiff upper lip.

Sincerely,
J. Rutherford Pinckney,
President

ART NEWS.

DO YOU HAVE an extra steam turbine taking up space in the basement? Installation artist Eli "Bonkers" Johnson needs it for a new work opening this fall, *Autumn Leaves*. No compensation can be offered, but a contingent of students from the Creative and Performing Arts High School will remove the object from your basement free of charge.

The Duck Hollow Museum of Art would like to remind patrons of the "no snickering" policy in the contemporary galleries on the second floor. Museum security guards will strictly enforce this policy, and are authorized to use force.

An investigation has determined that custodial staff were responsible for more than $350,000 worth of damage to *Another Man's Treasure*, the work by Spanish artist Luis Goya y Hoya y Carambolla in the Mattress Factory that was reported vandalized yesterday. According to the curator, one of the staff explained, "When I see garbage on the floor, I sweep it up." Staff are working with Mr. Goya y Hoya y Carambolla to restore the work to something close to its original condition. A call for grapefruit rinds, eggshells, and half-empty Chinese takeout containers has gone out to the community, with a gratifying response so far. Meanwhile, a press release from the Mattress Factory states that "philistines" on the custodial staff have been replaced.

NERGAL-SHAREZER THE RABMAG'S
ASTROLOGICAL PROGNOSTICATIONS.

Leo. You are struck today by how trivial your life has been so far, and resolve to accomplish something important beginning tomorrow. You are also struck by a falling piano, rendering your resolution redundant.

Virgo. The piano that falls on you today is worth $35,682, which by a bizarre coincidence is all you declared out of the $23,182,914.33 you made on the commodities market last year.

Libra. You just miss being crushed by a falling piano in the 800 block of Penn Avenue, which makes the piano in the 900 block all the more amusing, from a cosmic point of view.

Scorpio. There is a large wad of chewing gum on the sidewalk on Wood Street just past Weldin's. You notice it well in time to give it a wide berth and step into the shadow of a plummeting piano.

Sagittarius. A tall, dark stranger with a mysterious past seems to be trying to signal you. He is pointing upward with every sign of extreme agitation. You wave back.

Capricorn. The stars had a message for you in Morse code, but the connection was interrupted. They had spelled out S-T-E-I-N-W-, and then stopped.

Aquarius. Life has taught you many lessons. It has taught you to look twice before crossing the street. It has taught you to fasten your seat belt even for a short trip. It has not taught you to look up whenever you pass luxury condominiums popular with musicians. Too bad about that.

Pisces. Remember how you hated piano lessons when you were a kid? Remember how your mother told you the piano wasn't going to kill you? She was wrong.

Aries. Some say that Sergei Rachmaninoff knew his way around a piano better than any other man in the past century. Today you will become even more intimately acquainted with a Steinway Model O.

Taurus. Today is the day you've been dreading for weeks. You can't think of any way out of that meeting at 3 p.m., and you're sure you're going to make a fool of yourself. Well, the stars have good news and bad news.

Gemini. With Venus in the house of Saxe-Coburg-Gotha, today would be an excellent opportunity to begin a new relationship, or to make a fresh start in an old one. Too bad about that piano.

Cancer. You are about to have the worst day you have ever had in your job as shift supervisor at the Excelsior Piano & Organ Hoisting Co., Inc.

UNENFORCEABLE LAWS.

MANY OF THE laws on the books in states and local jurisdictions are unenforceable: that is, they would never be upheld if appeal were made to a higher court. That they remain in theoretical force is usually due either to inertia or to some strong political interest in the legislative bodies.

In Dagsboro, Delaware, it is illegal to teach a horse to play backgammon.

In Utah, a man who mentions the name of Brigham Young without removing his hat may be fined 75¢ for the first offense and an even dollar for each offense thereafter.

The Pope is not permitted to set foot in the borough of Dormont, Penna.

Since 2003, citizens of Arkansas have been required to report suspected French people to the state police, on penalty of being declared French themselves.

In Brattleboro, Vt., he that hath two coats is required to impart to him that hath none.

A law dating from 1873 in Oneonta, N.Y., makes each impure thought a separate felony.

The police in Mason City, Iowa, are empowered to shoot mattress salesmen on sight.

THE CARTER COTTERED CRANK

Is the Cream of the Crop In Cottered Cranks.

The Carter Cottered Crank Corporation of Caudle, Colorado, Carefully Crafts Each Cottered Crank. The Carter Cottered Crank Cannot Crack, Crease, or Crumble.

For a Finer Fit and Finish, the Carter Cottered Crank Corporation Suggests Stanley Stainless Spun Steel Safety Sprockets. Stanley Stainless Spun Steel Safety Sprockets Surpass the Strictest Safety Standards.

MEMORANDUM.

TO: All Employees
FROM: The President
RE: Corporate Personhood

Doubtless you are all aware that, under the laws of the United States, as interpreted by no less an authority than the Supreme Court (which I gather has some influence in these matters), a Corporation is legally a person, with all the rights and privileges attached to that exalted position, although (curiously enough) none of the responsibilities.

The Schenectady Small Arms & Biscuit Co., Inc., is proud to carry on a long tradition of corporate personhood, or "corporate Persephone," as my spelling checker would like me to write, and I hope you all find that as amusing as I did. We have exercised our right to freedom of speech, for example, by bribing every politician in the Capital District, with the happy result that cookie-control legislation has been defeated every time it was proposed in Albany.

But what good are all our triumphs if the corporation is not treated as a real person? As a legal person, has it not legal feelings? Why, then, is the corporation never invited to any of your children's birthday parties? After all, the corporation, through its representatives (namely the board and myself), likes ice cream and cake as well as anybody.

The next time your child has a birthday, don't forget to set a place for the Schenectady Small Arms & Biscuit Co., Inc. You'll be helping a corporation that means a great deal to all of us feel more like the real person our Supreme Court has said it is. And, in return, the Corporation is inviting you all to its 125th birthday party next Tuesday during your lunch break. Don't forget to bring a suitable gift.

With Love,

J. Rutherford Pinckney,

President.

THE BOY WHO CRIED WOLF.
From *Dr. Boli's Fables for Children
Who Are Too Old to Believe in Fables.*

ONCE THERE WAS a boy who had a keen pair of eyes and a partic-ularly loud and piercing voice, so he was employed by a syndicate of sheep-owners to watch over their flock. "And if you see a wolf among the sheep," the leader of the syndicate told him, "you shout 'Wolf! Wolf!' at the top of your lungs."

The boy solemnly swore that he would keep a careful eye out and warn everyone the moment he saw a wolf, and he went to work watch-ing the sheep with unflagging vigilance.

He had been watching most of the afternoon with nothing to report, when suddenly a wolf sprang out of the underbrush and, to his horror, began devouring one of the sheep.

"Wolf! Wolf!" the boy cried at the top of his lungs.

Immediately the leader of the syndicate came running.

"Look here, boy," he said sternly, as the wolf continued his meal, "what are you trying to do? Do you want the whole village to think we don't know how to take care of our sheep?"

"But the wolf is eating them!"

"That's no excuse for such an unseemly ruckus. You ought to be ashamed of yourself." And the leader of the syndicate turned and walked away, leaving the wolf to eat mutton until he was satisfied.

The next day the boy was in position again, and once again the wolf leaped out of the brush and began tearing a sheep to pieces.

"Wolf! Wolf!" the boy cried in his piercing soprano.

The leader of the syndicate came running even faster than he had the previous day.

"Now, what did I tell you?" he demanded angrily. "You're making the whole village think there are wolves about! Do you think that makes them feel secure?"

"But the wolf is right there," the boy explained.

"I don't want to be bothered with details! Now, not another peep from you, or there will be serious consequences." And he turned and stomped away angrily, once again leaving the wolf to eat sheep until he could eat no more.

The next day, the boy was in his place, and once again the wolf leaped out of the shrubbery and began gobbling up sheep.

The boy was not at all certain what to do. He seriously considered just letting the wolf go about his business unmolested. But in the end he remembered that he had sworn a solemn oath to watch over the sheep, and he did what he knew was his duty.

"Wolf! Wolf!" the boy cried.

This time the leader of the syndicate simply called the police and had the boy arrested, and he is now serving six years in juvenile detention for disturbing the peace.

The wolf, meanwhile, ate all the sheep at his leisure; but the members of the syndicate decided that they had never liked sheep very much and were better off without them.

MORAL: *A comfortable lie beats immoderate truth any old day.*

SUMMER BLOCKBUSTER.

WELL, J. M., it was a great idea to buy the rights to *Le Sang d'un poete*, cause everybody knows it's a total classic. I mean, who doesn't want to see a remake of that one? And we think we've got a swell idea for turning it into a summer blockbuster that'll just blow everything else out of the water. We'll call it *Talk to the Hand.*

All we had to do was update the story a little bit for the twenty-first century. Like, instead of a painter, we make the hero a comic-book artist. So it's about this guy who draws comic books, right? Cause everyone likes comic books. And he has a crush on this cute girl, but he can never speak to her, because he's a shy artist type. She'd really like to go out with him, but he doesn't know it. That's romance, see? You gotta have romance.

So one day he draws a mouth on a close-up of one of his superhero characters, and he doesn't like it, right? So he rubs off the mouth with his hand. And now the mouth is on his hand, and it starts talking! Just like in the original movie. But fans will love how we've updated it, cause now we'll do it with CGI. And here's where you have to hold on to your hat, cause this is where it just blows you away: see, the mouth talks in jive talk, right? You know, like colored people do. We can get Eddie Murphy for the voice. Can you imagine how the kids will love that? It'll be colossal! The mouth will be the big breakout character in the movie, see.

So the mouth is always mouthing off—get it?—and the guy doesn't know what to do, cause the mouth on his hand is always saying the darnedest things. And he can't let anyone know it's there, cause it's like there's this mouth. On his hand. I mean, that makes him a freak, right? So, like, whenever the mouth says something outrageous, he has to pretend that he said it, except he has to pretend he was trying to say something else. It's hilarious! The jokes just write themselves.

And the mouth sees—well, knows, anyway, cause it isn't an eye, it's a mouth—that the artist guy wants to get together with the cute girl, so the mouth starts doing everything to make him get together with her, and it's just hilarious. And think of all the jokes about where the mouth is when he puts his hand here or there! We're going to have this totally hilarious hand-washing scene in the kitchen.

But meanwhile the FBI is after the artist guy, because they know about the mouth and they think the guy is an alien or a mutant or something. We haven't worked that part out yet. The main thing is that he's being chased by the FBI for *some* reason, so there's conflict. And if he gets chased, then we can blow stuff up, cause kids need things to blow up in a movie.

And the girl gets involved too, cause he has to go to her apartment to hide, or maybe the FBI thinks she's his girlfriend and goes after her, or something. Anyway, they go on the lam together, and she finds out about the mouth, and she and the mouth are like buddies, and there's a happy ending, but he's still got the mouth on his hand, so we can do the sequel in 2017.

So that's it, J. M. It's the movie Cocteau would have made if he'd had a hundred fifty million dollars to work with. Totally brilliant idea to buy the rights. You're a genius, J. M. You know that, right? Course you do.

POPULAR MISCONCEPTIONS ABOUT THE CIVIL WAR,
By Dr. Ambrose Hinge, Ph.D.,
Associate Professor of History at Duck Hollow University.

MISUNDERSTANDINGS AND MISCONCEPTIONS are distressingly prevalent in discussions of the Civil War. I have been given space to clear up only a few of them, but my upcoming book, *The "Civil" War Was Really Quite Rude*, is recommended to any readers who wish to delve further into this dark period in our history.

Misconception: The Civil War was fought to free the slaves.

Fact: The governments of the seceding states, which fired the first shots in the conflict, explicitly intended to prevent the slaves from being freed. This is a matter of public record.

Misconception: The Southerners fought to protect states' rights.

Fact: The Southerners' most frequent accusation against the North was that individual Northern states had passed laws that prevented the effective enforcement of the federal Fugitive Slave Act.

Misconception: The Civil War was very romantic.

Fact: It has been historically documented that, far from being the stuff of romance, the Civil War was dirty and dangerous, and several people were actually hurt.

Misconception: The Civil War was unavoidable in the conditions of the time.

Fact: It has been conclusively demonstrated that both sides could have avoided the war altogether by not shooting at each other.

Misconception: Brother fought brother on the battlefields of the Civil War.

Fact: In fewer than 0.1% of cases were siblings divided in their allegiance, making it statistically very improbable that one brother would encounter another fighting on the opposite side in any given battle.

Misconception: Southerners fought for a worthy and noble "Lost Cause."

Fact: The so-called "Lost Cause" was actually found under Jefferson Davis' desk when Union troops entered Richmond in 1865. He had been using it to prop up one of the legs. It had therefore never really been lost at all.

Misconception: The Civil War succeeded in freeing the slaves.

Fact: Most adult Americans spend eight or more hours a day at the mercy of the arbitrary whims of an employer.

CANINE THEOLOGY.

THE GODS PROVIDE food and open the back door, but otherwise they are not very bright.

They arc divinc because they walk upright and have opposable thumbs. With those advantages, the canine race would be divine as well.

Earnest prayer is required to make the food appear in the dish. It sometimes takes hours for the gods to get the message, which is why it is advisable for dogs to start praying several hours before dawn.

The loudest prayer is the most effective.

The gods are not omniscient, but somehow they always know that it was not one of them who chewed up the bedspread.

Sometimes it is necessary to chew up the bedspread, even at the risk of divine wrath.

Whereas dogs communicate by leaving postings on tree trunks and fire hydrants, the gods communicate primarily by making variously modulated sounds come out of their mouths.

The divine language is far more complicated than it needs to be to express the two fundamental concepts "FOOD" and "OUTSIDE."

It is possible for dogs to understand some of the divine language, but it is advisable not to let the gods know the extent of our understanding.

One of the words the gods speak most frequently is "NO." We have no idea what this means, but canine theologians are confident that they are close to decoding it.

When taking a god for a walk, it is necessary to be somewhat forceful with the leash. Left to his own devices, a god will walk right past all the interesting postings without reading them.

When the gods summon us, it is always best to ascertain first whether they have a treat to offer before obeying their summons. In that way we train them to be good and attentive divinities who always come through with the goods when they want worship.

ENTERTAINING AT PARTIES.
No. 1.—Acting Out Idioms & Proverbs.

MUCH DELIGHTFUL AMUSEMENT may be had at parties by dividing your guests into actors and spectators and playing this very amusing game. The actors are given a series of idioms and proverbs, which they are required to act out in pantomime; the spectators must attempt to guess which idiom or proverb is represented. A few examples will suffice to demonstrate how the game may be played:

A player walks into the center of the room leading a live elephant. He stands still in the center of the room and attempts to persuade the elephant to do the same. Idiom: *The elephant in the room.*

An actor walks in carrying a battery-operated alarm clock from which the battery has been removed. He sets the clock before him and glances at his watch (which is set to the correct time), then at the face of the clock. He repeats these actions until the watch and the alarm clock at last read the same time; then he jumps up and down excitedly, pointing to the clock. Then he sits and waits twelve more hours, repeating the same actions as before. Proverb: *A stopped clock is right twice a day.*

Two actors enter, one carrying a tray of hors d'oeuvres. The one with the tray attempts to place some of the food in the mouth of the other, who bites down on the first actor's fingers, causing howls of pain. Idiom: *Bite the hand that feeds you.*

Nine actors are suspended by a fraying strip of fabric over a cauldron of boiling oil. A tenth appears with a needle and thread and sews the fraying fabric to prevent it from tearing. Proverb: *A stitch in time saves nine.*

An actor opens a large sack suspended above the spectators, releasing a number of animals (easily obtained from a local animal shelter) to land on the heads of the amused and delighted audience. Idiom: *Raining cats and dogs.*

An actor leads a leopard to the center of the room and begins to scrub the animal with a sponge, giving up when he or the leopard has had enough of the charade, and pointing at the leopard's fur while sadly shaking his head, if it is still attached to his body. Proverb: *A leopard cannot change his spots.*

An actor abruptly stands and leaves the room. He never comes back, and eventually the rest of the guests forget about him. Proverb: *Out of sight, out of mind.*

"But I says it's that transcendental unity of apperception wot started Kant down the wrong road altogether, d'ye see?"

NERGAL-SHAREZER THE RABMAG
INTERPRETS YOUR DREAMS.

Dear Mr. the Rabmag: Last night I dreamt I dwelt in marble halls, with vassals and serfs at my side; and, of all who assembled within those walls, that I was the hope and the pride. I had riches too great to count—could boast of a high ancestral name. But I also dreamt, which pleased me most, that you loved me still the same. What do you think it means? —Sincerely, Arline.

Dear Madam: Doubtless this dream represents a dim memory of your tragic origin story, and it is likely that you are well on your way to becoming a supervillain, if indeed you are not one already. The one consoling observation is the last part of the dream, which suggests that you may also be mad. Most supervillains are mad, and their madness invariably leads them to overstep the bounds of prudence in the execution of their diabolical plots. Although you will handily outwit the local police, and the entire United Nations will cower prostrate at your feet, it should be a relatively simple matter for the nearest costumed hero to foil your plot to destroy the world. You need not worry yourself too much about that, however: although you will appear to have perished in the blazing inferno that consumes your lair, future sequels will reveal that you survived by means of some exceedingly implausible plot contrivance.

HAPPY CRAFTY TIME.

HELLO, HAPPY CHILDREN! Did you miss your Aunt Lizzy? Well, I'm back, and once again it's Happy Crafty Time!

Today we're going to do something special. We're going to make a birdhouse for all our little birdie friends. When we're done, the little birdies will have a nicer house than your Aunt Lizzy has, not that that's saying much.

Now, the first thing we need for a birdhouse is some wood. And we're in luck! I'll bet there's wood all over your house. Like the table in your dining room, or the dresser in Mommy and Daddy's bedroom —they're probably made of wood! Just like this French provincial coffee table I found in the studio next door where they do the Morning View show. All you need is to get the wood out of them. And that's why I brought this chainsaw. Can you say "Husqvarna"? I don't even know if I'm pronouncing it right, but it sure does the job. All we have to do is [- - - - *inaudible* - - - -] and there we are—all the wood we need for our birdhouse!

Now the next step is to glue these pieces together so that they form a birdhouse. All you'll need is some of that instant-stick super-glue. But you have to be careful with it. Otherwise you might end up accidentally gluing your little brother to his bicycle seat, and while that would be very funny, you might get in trouble if you're stupid enough to get caught.

So here we are! Isn't this a pretty birdhouse? This is one I bought down at the Metro Mart, because all the birdhouses I tried to make looked like a pile of lumber glued together by a drunk.

Well, that's all we have time for today on Happy Crafty Time. And just remember, children, do your best in school, because you don't want to end up in a job you despise where you can't get out of your contract unless they fire you while you watch the people you grew up with land all the cool shows where they get to interview the mayor or dress up like a vampire and introduce scary movies or even cook stuff guys like to eat and you're stuck in the same rut year after year until all you dream of at night is scissors and construction paper and you can't get a date because people think you're some kind of cross between a nun and a fluffy stuffed bunny. That's all for now! Tomorrow, unless they fire me, I'm going to show you some really fun things you can do with just an ordinary gas stove. So till next time, have a happy crafty day!

MEMORANDUM.

TO: All Employees
FROM: The President
RE: Quarterly Dividend

All of us here at the Schenectady Small Arms & Biscuit Co., Inc., have experienced some anxiety since the 20% layoffs last month. It is useless to pretend otherwise. You may think that, in my position of exalted responsibility, I would have nothing to worry about, but I assure you that that is not the case. There are days when I think that if I hear any more sniveling from the cubicles I shall simply "lose it," to use a colorful vernacular term, although I am not sure what "it" is supposed to be, and why I should be unduly distressed about losing "it" when I could just send my administrative assistant out to get another of "it."

I must tell you candidly that the layoffs were not without stress for your executive team. In order to produce the maximum cost savings for our quarterly numbers, it was necessary to rid ourselves of the most expensive 20% of the workforce (exclusive of management, of course): that is, the workers who, by their intelligence, hard work, and loyalty, had earned the highest salaries and the most in bonuses. It required actual work on one of those math boxes with the numbered buttons to identify these people. In fact, it was exactly the sort of work that would usually be assigned to the best and brightest in the company, but for obvious reasons it had to be done without their knowledge.

Today, however, I am sure you will be delighted to hear that our hard work in identifying and firing the overachievers has paid off handsomely, and with the money we saved on salaries and benefits we have been able to increase our quarterly dividend from 8¢ to 9¢. Not only does this demonstrate our confidence to the stock market, but it also has a direct effect on executive compensation, which is highly motivational for your executive team.

I wish once again to convey to you how much the Schenectady Small Arms & Biscuit Co., Inc., values the intelligence, hard work, and loyalty of its employees, especially in the upcoming quarter, during which we hope to be able to raise the dividend to 10¢, thus reaching the double digits for the first time and sending a strong message to stockholders that we have their best interests at heart. To do so will require dedication, perseverance, and another 20% cutback in the workforce by the same method as before. However, with the information you have now, you should be well aware of what you have to do to be one of the lucky 80%.

With Warmest Regards,
J. Rutherford Pinckney,
President

SECRET SOCIETY OF THE ONYX PERSIMMON.

Dear Mr. Occupant,

Your time has come.

We want you to be prosperous. We want you to be rich—a member of that secret society of the wealthy and successful who are the true masters of the world.

The fact is, we know quite a bit about you, Mr. Occupant. We believe in you. We believe in your ability to stand out from the crowd. We believe that you will grow so successful that you will be one of our most valuable acquaintances.

That's why we have a special secret volume prepared for you, Mr. Current Occupant, and all your descendants.

Yes, that's right. We're so sure that this secret volume will become a treasured Occupant family heirloom that we've ordered our printers to inscribe it not just to you, but to the entire Occupant family dynasty. Generations of Occupants will grow rich beyond the dreams of avarice —all on the strength of the secrets revealed in this book.

Who are we?

We are the Secret Society of the Onyx Persimmon. We are the wealthy, the successful, the influential, the ultra rich.

We're just flabbergasted by how much promise we see in you. You should be overwhelmed and excited. Your life is about to change completely. You're about to make the great leap from mediocrity to excellence. You're about to embark on a journey of unbelievable good fortune. You're about to reap rewards beyond anything you could possibly imagine. You're about to buy our book.

This book isn't offered to just anybody. In fact, your special volume is already reserved for you and your immediate family—but no one else. Yours is Limited Heirloom Edition No. 6,004,027,628. Only your book bears this number.

Just fill out the form included with this mailing, send it back in the enclosed business-reply envelope, and wire your payment to our numbered account in the Cayman Islands. Your book, and your membership in the Secret Society of the Onyx Persimmon, will be on its way the next day.

Look around you, Mr. Occupant. Say farewell to your poverty, your mediocrity, your ordinary surroundings. The dawn of the Occupant family dynasty is at hand.

Sincerely,
"January"
General Secretary of the Cabal of the Twelve
Secret Society of the Onyx Persimmon

THE ADVENTURES OF SIR MONTAGUE BLASTOFF, INTERPLANETARY SPACE DRAGOON.

ANNOUNCER. And now Malt-O-Cod, the only malt food drink flavored with real cod-liver oil, proudly presents...

(*Music: Fanfare*)

ANNOUNCER. The Adventures of Sir Montague Blastoff, Interplanetary Space Dragoon!

(*Music: Theme, in and under for...*)

ANNOUNCER. Today we find Sir Montague positively bubbling with excitement as Colonel Wilhelmina Darling arrives at his door.

SIR MONTAGUE. I say, Colonel, are you ready to meet William Shakespeare?

COL. DARLING. Oh, Monty, I'm positively bubbling with excitement!

SIR MONTAGUE. Are you really? What an extraordinary coincidence! Well, here we are, the first man and the first woman ever in the history of the world to travel through time!

COL. DARLING. I can hardly believe we're actually going to do it!

SIR MONTAGUE. Are you sure you're up for it, my dear? The experiment is not without its risks, you know.

COL. DARLING. I may be only nineteen and ravishingly beautiful, but I am also a colonel in the 58th Interplanetary Space Dragoons. I do not know the meaning of the word "fear."

SIR MONTAGUE. Well, you should have said something, my dear. You know you can borrow my dictionary any time you like. Now, just through these doors here, and we'll enter the Temporal Displacement Chamber.

(*Sound: Echoing footsteps.*)

COL. DARLING. Look! There's somebody already in there!

SIR MONTAGUE. Well, that's highly irregular. I say in there! Are you aware that this is a restricted area?

SIR MONTAGUE (*distant*). Oh, yes, quite, of course. Filled out the paperwork myself.

COL. DARLING. Good grief, Monty! It's us!

SIR MONTAGUE. Is this some sort of horrible malfunction of the machinery?

SIR MONTAGUE (*approaching*). Only a bit of a hiccup, really. Nothing much to worry about. We've just returned a little before we left.

COL. DARLING. Wilhelmina, you have a bit of spinach in your teeth.

COL. DARLING. Good grief! Why didn't Monty tell me?

COL. DARLING. He never notices these things.

COL. DARLING. No, he doesn't, does he?

SIR MONTAGUE. But, I say! This means the experiment was a success!

SIR MONTAGUE. Oh, rather! Went swimmingly, except for this little awkward bit at the end.

SIR MONTAGUE. Or at the beginning.

SIR MONTAGUE. Yes, quite. See your point. Jolly amusing when you think about it, isn't it?

COL. DARLING. So you've already met Shakespeare?

COL. DARLING. He's not all he's cracked up to be.

SIR MONTAGUE. Well, you two had better be off. If you don't

leave now, we'll never have gone at all, which would be rather embar-rassing. Not to mention the paperwork.

SIR MONTAGUE. Yes, we'd best be off.

COL. DARLING. It was nice meeting me.

COL. DARLING. Yes, I'll be seeing you in my mirror.

SIR MONTAGUE. Well, that was a bit odd, but here we are. Are you ready?

COL. DARLING. I'm always ready for anything when I'm with you, Monty.

SIR MONTAGUE. Jolly good. Then I'll just pull this lever, and...

(*Sound: Loud electrical hum.*)

SIR MONTAGUE. Here we are in Elizabethan England! And according to this Poet Triangulator in my hand, William Shakespeare should be in that house over there.

COL. DARLING. You mean the one with the long line of people coiled up in front of it?

SIR MONTAGUE. Yes, that's the one. I say, you over there. Is Mr. William Shakespeare available?

GUARD. Back of the line, you two.

SIR MONTAGUE. But perhaps you misunderstand. We only want to see Mr. Shakespeare.

GUARD. Do you have any idea how many time travelers show up here every day to get a glimpse of Shakespeare at work? He hardly has time to write with all the visitors he gets from future centuries. Line forms here. Five minutes each with the poet. Estimated wait time two hours thirty-five minutes from this point. Souvenir shop after the poet.

SIR MONTAGUE. Well, Colonel, I suppose there's nothing for it but to stand here and wait. Still, two and a half hours is a small price to pay for meeting the greatest English poet who ever lived. I suppose we can wait.

COL. DARLING. I'm not so sure.

SIR MONTAGUE. Oh, come now, my dear, let's just have a little patience. It won't be as long as all that.

COL. DARLING. Monty, I know I should have thought of this before we left, but...

(*Music: Theme, in and under for...*)

ANNOUNCER. Will Sir Montague and Colonel Darling succeed in meeting William Shakespeare, or will Colonel Darling have to step out of line to use the facilities? Will they return in time to meet themselves along the way? Will next week's episode be an exact repeat of this week's? Don't miss next week's exciting episode: Sir Montague Blastoff and the Infinite Loop! Till then, kids, remember to bug your parents every day until they buy you Malt-O-Cod. It's the only malt food drink with the rich, satisfying flavor of real cod-liver oil, now with the exclusive Sir Montague Blastoff perpetual calendar in every package. It's the malt food drink that's brain food—Malt-O-Cod!

(*Music: In full, then out.*)

ARE YOU DEAD? You may be eligible to participate in a study being conducted by the Monongahela Valley Society for Psychical Research. Weekly seances are conducted at the Society's offices on Eighth Avenue in Munhall above Ferd's Pizza. Three raps on our round table will be considered an expression of interest. Please rap distinctly, so as to distinguish your communication from the ordinary commercial activities of Ferd. A small stipend will be paid to your estate on completion of the study. Monongahela Valley Society for Psychical Research, Munhall.

DR. BOLI'S LIBRARY OF LOST BOOKS.

On the Insufficiency of Grace, by the Rev. Dr. Carolus Fraile.

THE RUMOR THAT the Rev. Dr. Carolus Fraile, a respected Lutheran pastor at St. Lydia's in Esplen, had written a manuscript treatise "On the Insufficiency of Grace" caused much consternation in the synod office. Was Dr. Fraile a heretic? It was not in the nature of Lutherans even to ask such a question, yet the subject was too close to the heart of Lutheran doctrine to ignore. Indeed, the sufficiency and necessity of grace were, as the whispers in the synod office said, the very foundations of Lutheran doctrine. In all his sermons and his writing, Dr. Fraile had given every indication of orthodoxy. Could such a man have written a work with so provocative a title?

Soon the existence of the manuscript was positively confirmed by Miss Sarah Nebb, an elderly sexton who, while dusting in the pastor's office, found it necessary to move some of the pastor's personal papers, and accidentally read a good many of them. She had not succeeded in accidentally reading "On the Insufficiency of Grace" before the pastor unexpectedly returned, but there could be no doubt that she had seen the title.

As the known existence of the manuscript was already causing some scandal in the synod, the matter was brought up before the Standing Committee on Doctrine, which met the second Thursday of every month in a special room without chairs at the Palace Inn. For the first time in the recorded history of the Committee, the word "heresy" was mentioned in a regular meeting. After some debate, it was agreed that no adequate definition of "heresy" was available to the Committee, which therefore referred the matter to the Committee on the Clergy for any necessary investigation.

This Committee met twice a year at the Synod offices, so it was some months before the matter could be brought up. When the Committee did meet, it was unanimously agreed that the question of Dr. Fraile's manuscript was causing unnecessary scandal in the synod; and that, on the other hand, Dr. Fraile himself was a pastor of hitherto irreproachable reputation. It would be best, the Committee agreed, to interrogate Dr. Fraile personally, in a friendly and informal manner, without causing any undue uproar. Pastor Anna Strassenbahn was given the responsibility of conducting the interview, for which no particular parameters were specified.

When the committee met again six months later, Pastor Strassenbahn reported that Dr. Fraile was a very nice person, and that he seemed very sincere, although it had been very difficult to get an appointment with him—a difficulty he attributed to his overburdened secretary. When pressed, she admitted that she had not specifically brought up the subject of the manuscript, thinking that it would be somewhat indecorous to mention that its existence had become known when Dr. Fraile had made no effort to put it before the public. The Committee agreed that Pastor Strassenbahn had acted with becoming decorum, and referred the matter to the Committee on Missions, which met every other year at the Sideling Hill Resort and Spa.

When, after nineteen months, the matter was brought up before the Committee on Missions, the members expressed some bewilderment. They agreed that the matter was not within the purview of the Committee on Missions, and referred it to the West Central Division Council, as the governing body with immediate authority over the congregation of St. Lydia's.

The Council met every four years at a different member church, but construction at St. Aquila's caused the next meeting to be canceled. It was therefore seven years before the matter could be brought up before the Council, which by a curious coincidence was meeting at St. Lydia's that year. As Dr. Fraile was himself acting as host, it was deemed inappropriate to discuss the matter at that meeting, so the question was referred to the Synod Office.

At that time, however, the bishop was on an extended tour of the sister synod in Madagascar, so he was unavailable for the next few years, and the bishop's assistant was unwilling to make a decision of such import on his own. Three years later, the bishop unexpectedly resigned to pursue a career as a professional lacrosse player, and it was some years before a new bishop could be chosen.

Eventually, however, the new bishop was installed, and the matter of Dr. Fraile brought up before him. By this time, Dr. Fraile himself had died of chicken pox at the age of 112, but by means of a politely worded letter the bishop obtained permission from his heirs to examine Dr. Fraile's personal papers.

When the manuscript was finally received, the bishop sent it to Dr. Theodore Hogwood, president of the Duck Hollow Theological Seminary, with a request that he examine the thesis and summarize the doctrines expressed in it.

In only a few months, the distinguished theologian was able to forward his report.

The manuscript began, said the report, with an invocation, and then a number of relevant quotations from the Psalms. It then proceeded to address the St. Lydia's church council directly with a statement of the main thesis: that Miss Grace Pfolder, the secretary at St. Lydia's, was not capable of handling by herself the weighty labor that had been thrust upon her by the gratifying growth of the parish; that it was absolutely necessary to hire an assistant to the secretary, as Grace by herself was entirely insufficient. The remainder of the manuscript was devoted to illustrative examples, illuminated by similar events from Old Testament history, and amplified by citations from the epistles of St. Paul. There was nothing, he said, counter to traditional Lutheran doctrine in the manuscript. Thus the matter was brought to a gratifying close, and, as the bishop himself remarked, the process (as he called it) was vindicated.

Since that time the manuscript has not been seen, but that may be largely because no one has looked for it.

"It's all very well for you to say your regiment leaves at dawn, but your mother tells me you're actually a bellhop." (Page 1227.)

GROUNDHOG DAY AND SIMILAR TRADITIONS.

THE MOST ILLUSTRIOUS Punxsutawney Phil, though he is the best known, is by no means the only prognosticating rodent whose services are called upon by the human inhabitants of his region. Many other rodents around the world are also well known for their predictions:

In Yeehaw Junction, Fla., Yeehaw Yekaterina, a fox squirrel, predicts the number of tanker trucks that will pass on Route 441 each August 28 with astonishing accuracy.

In Bom Dispacho, Brazil, Deodoro the Capybara advises the town commission on zoning matters.

In Hard Bargain, Bahamas, if Hard-Bargain Hattie the Hutia hears the ocean's roar on Arbor Day, it means six more months of instability in the commodities market.

In Ouea, Djibouti, if Ouea Omar the Speke's Pectinator leaves footprints in the sand more than 28 mm apart, there will be a warm Ramadan.

In Litchfield, Minnesota, if Litchfield Louie the Plains Pocket Gopher scratches behind his right ear, run like blazes.

In Llanarthney, Wales, Llanarthney Lloyd the Bank Vole was for many years a secret investments advisor to Barclays, until his association with the bank was revealed in testimony before the House of Lords (source: Daily Mail, "Filthy Rodent Broke Our Banks," Jan. 16, 2009).

ARE YOU ANNOYING, loudmouthed, bad-tempered, obnoxious, mean, or insufferable? Enjoy social gatherings with like-minded individuals every Thursday at 7:30 p.m. Rude Fellows Lodge No. 749, Monessen.

TRADITIONAL REMEDIES FOR HICCUPS.

TAKE ONE TEASPOON of sugar and wave it under the nose repeatedly until the hiccups cease.

Recite the Gettysburg Address backwards, translating into Finnish as you go. When you reach the beginning, the hiccups will be gone.

Hold your head in your hands and rock back and forth for several minutes, moaning.

Contract a more serious disease, thus giving the body something else to entertain itself with.

Pinch the upper part of the nose, tilt the head backward, and count to thirty-seven. If you forget to stop and go beyond thirty-seven, begin again.

Play "Rose of Washington Square" on the banjo as fast as you possibly can.

Read Lord Lytton's *Devereux*.

Sneeze repeatedly. This strategy usually takes the hiccups by surprise.

CHINESE ASTROLOGY,
by Nergal-Sharezer the Rabmag.

WESTERN ASTROLOGY IS based on the idea that the date of
one's birth, which comes about once a year in an unending cycle, de-
termines one's destiny. Chinese astrology, on the other hand, postu-
lates that the year of one's birth is the determining element.

Nergal-Sharezer the Rabmag has great respect for the ancient wisdom of the Celestial Empire, and believes that the mere fact that
these two systems are mutually exclusive should not be taken as evidence that they are not both true.

The twelve years of the Chinese astrological cycle are named for
various animals. After twelve years, the cycle repeats, on the assumption that most people have short memories and will not notice. To determine the name of the year in which you were born, simply divide
the current year by the year of your birth, and then look up the result
in Nergal-Sharezer the Rabmag's Handy Chinese Astrology Reference Book, available for $19.95 from better booksellers everywhere.

Ox. For your whole life you will carry the stigma of an irregular plural.
Marry a Lion late in life. We mean a person born in the year of the
lion, not that you should marry an actual lion, which the surgeon general has determined could lead to serious injury.

Dragon. You are noble and beautiful. Generous by nature, you show fearless courage in every undertaking. You are trusted and admired by every living being. You are entirely mythological, which explains your other attributes.

Lion. You are immoderately proud, with a tendency to lick yourself for hours.

Snake. Sly, somewhat sinister but seldom slimy, slightly short. A sucker for sibilant sounds.

Marmoset. You have an aptitude for repetitive clerical work. Marry a snake early in life. Not a person born in the year of the snake, but an actual reptile.

Cockroach. You will live a short and miserable life and no one will love you. Enemies are the Ox, the Dragon, the Lion, the Snake, the Marmoset, the Spotted Phalanger, the Peccary, the Gnu, the Ocelot, the Tapir, the Squirrel, and the Pennsylvania Turnpike Commission.

Spotted Phalanger. You are a nocturnal marsupial, carrying your young in your pouch and hanging from tree limbs by your prehensile tail. You feed on fruit, buds, meat, and eggs.

Peccary. You have a placid disposition and are inclined to melancholy. Your artistic side is wisely repressed most of the time. The ox is your friend, but he never calls anymore.

Gnu. Your parents are to blame for most of what will happen to you.

Ocelot. Your fine moral sense will keep you unemployed most of your life. Beware of the Spotted Phalanger, because if you see one you are in New Guinea and therefore lost.

Tapir. Resilience is your best quality, and it is indeed just as well for you that you have great reserves of it to call upon.

Squirrel. Your innate intelligence and good sense render you impervious to all forms of quackery and nonsense, and Nergal-Sharezer the Rabmag wants nothing to do with you.

DR. BOLI'S LIBRARY OF LOST BOOKS
Caprodorus: Scythian Tale

ALTHOUGH ONLY SCATTERED fragments remain today, Caprodorus' *Scythian Tale* was one of the most popular Greek prose romances of the third century. From the many summaries, criticisms, pictorial representations, and character trading cards that have come down to us from antiquity, we can reconstruct the plot with surprising accuracy.

Theodore, a shepherd of Scythia, and Theodora, a shepherdess of the same address, declare their love for each other in frequent outbursts of song. But the flow of dactylic endearments is interrupted when a band of pirates, temporarily abandoning their maritime depredations to rustle a few sheep, invade the pasture and abduct Theodora, apparently misidentifying her cries for help as bleating. They leave Theodore for dead and depart for the high seas with their woolly cargo.

Theodore, however, is not dead, having merely stepped aside to answer a call of nature, or (according to the reading of Schleusegatter et al., 1931) the telephone. Informed by his remaining sheep of Theodora's abduction, he vows to become a pirate himself and join the pirate band that abducted Theodora, seeking the earliest opportunity to effect her rescue. This is apparently the best plan he can come up with.

The pirates having meanwhile discovered that Theodora is more woman than sheep, Theodora evades their advances by pretending to be Ethiopian and also mad. This ruse puzzles the pirates, and before they have time to resolve their confusion, their ship is ambushed by a band of forest bandits, who have temporarily set aside their life of sheep-rustling to try their hands at piracy. Taken by surprise, the pirates have no choice but to surrender their ship and cargo to the forest bandits, who then become pirates themselves, leaving the former pirates to become maritime forest bandits.

Theodora attempts to elude the new pirates with the same ruse that proved so successful with the former group; but she is foiled when she discovers that the pirates, formerly forest bandits, are all Ethiopian themselves, and most of them are quite mad.

Theodore, meanwhile, has come to the island of Rhodes, where he had been told he had the best chance of finding a pirate band willing to take on a new member with no previous references. Here he immediately falls among witches, who propose to turn him into a hedgehog. When he pleads for his life, however, the witches spare him, on the condition that he will present them with his head in a sack in exactly a year's time. Theodore readily agrees, being honest but not too bright. Upon his swearing a solemn oath, the witches put him in a small boat and give it a hard shove eastward.

Scarcely has Theodore departed when the pirate ship carrying Theodora, piloted as it is by former forest bandits with no experience on the high seas, smashes on the rocks off the shore of Rhodes. All the pirates are drowned, but Theodora, who knows how to wade, makes it to shore and immediately falls among the same witches who had threatened to turn Theodore into a hedgehog. The witches decide to try the same experiment on Theodora, but she makes the same agreement that Theodore made; and the witches place her in a similar small boat, giving it a hard shove to the west this time.

After many more adventures which it would be, and in fact was, tedious to relate, both Theodore and Theodora return to the island of Rhodes at the same time to fulfill their bargains. They fail to recognize each other, however, because they have both cut off their own heads and are carrying them in sacks to present to the witches. In a piece of droll comedy that was much talked about in Caprodorus' time, Theodore stumbles and Theodora trips over him, both dropping their heads on the ground. When they pick themselves up and dust themselves off, each picks up the wrong head and presents it to the witches. Furious, the witches restore their heads to their bodies and tell them to do it all over again and get it right this time.

But just as they are about to cut off their heads again, Theodore and Theodora recognize each other, and their moving reunion so affects the head witch that she sobbingly reveals that she is in fact Theodora's long-lost mother, who was abducted by pirates before Theodora was born. At that very moment comes a sudden attack by forest bandits, and you can imagine everyone's surprise when the bandits turn out to be none other than the original pirates who had abducted Theodora. Recognizing Theodora's mother the witch, the captain of the forest bandits reveals that he was the pirate who had abducted her all those years ago. A happy reunion is effected, and Theodora's mother and the bandit captain decide to open a souvenir shop on the beach. No one is quite sure what happens to Theodore and Theodora.

PROFESSIONAL PROFILES.

Randolph Bilwidge has 17 years of experience as a Psychic Healer, Total Personality Coordinator (TPC), Medical Astrologer, Street Sweeper, Reiki Master, and Methodist Minister. If you are looking for answers, Randy can tell you which questions to ask. If you need Reiki therapy, Randy is known throughout the tri-county area as the master with the gentlest non-touch. If you are in need of Psychic Healing, Randy has already rearranged your aura and charged your MasterCard account. You're welcome.

Mirabella Transom has created remarkable interior spaces for over 8 clients in a number of different states. She is currently offering her interior-decorating services at a greatly reduced rate as part of her mandated work-release program.

Marcus Aurelius Antoninus Augustus was Emperor of Rome for nearly twenty years. In spite of his busy imperial schedule, he found time during his reign to write a popular self-help book that has been translated into more than seventy languages. He successfully persecuted a considerable number of Christians. He is currently accepting applications from larger empires in need of a decisive but contemplative ruler.

Mildred Shuckles has worked for the Department of Sanitation since 1938. She is now interested in a career as a freelance garbage collector, and is currently accepting clients.

Ruthven Mophandle Heyser is a successful composer of orchestral and chamber works. He is best known for his rejection of Shoenberg's twelve-tone scale in favor of a series of different scales based on prime numbers. In 1994, he received the prestigious Charles Ives Medal for Advanced Cacophony. He is currently accepting commissions for advertising jingles.

CANINE TELEGRAPHY TRAINING. If your dog is a good speller, then he may be qualified for a career in CANINE TELEGRAPHY. A dire shortage of qualified human telegraph operators means that a well-trained dog is almost assured of a good position. We train by positive reinforcement, so that your dog will *want* to increase his speed to 20 words per minute or more. Bring your dog for a free aptitude test. Canine Telegraphic Academy of North Point Breeze, North Point Breeze.

Are You Subject to
Mood Swings?

Are you one of those unfortunate individuals who suffer from unpredictable changes of mood and demeanor? We would be most grateful if you would be so very kind as to help others with the same difficulties by participating in a trial of a new medication at the Duck Hollow University School of Medicine. It's a unique opportunity to show compassion for your fellow creatures and make something good come out of your own misfortune. After all, how hard can it be to move your fat carcass off the recliner and do something with your wasted life for once besides stuffing your disgusting face with Doritos? Just thinking about your wasted potential makes all of us here at the lab want to cry.

DUCK HOLLOW UNIVERSITY SCHOOL OF MEDICINE

The Latest in "Green" Technology!
ALTERNATIVE-ENERGY CLOTHES DRYER
Harness the Power of the Sun and Wind!

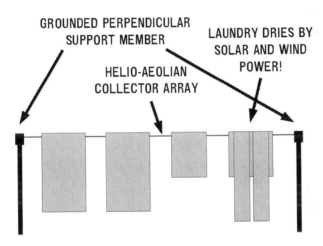

GROUNDED PERPENDICULAR SUPPORT MEMBER

HELIO-AEOLIAN COLLECTOR ARRAY

LAUNDRY DRIES BY SOLAR AND WIND POWER!

The patent-pending Xeromatic clothes-dryer uses *no gas* and *no electricity*, produces *no greenhouse gases*, and— best of all—actually benefits from global warming! The hotter it gets, the better it works! See your dealer today!

Advertisement.

Made in the USA
San Bernardino, CA
05 April 2017